D1554039

The
Perfect Gentleman's
Pocket Guide

Modern Secrets to Etiquette, Style and Charming Charisma

MICHAEL FERRERA

M World Media Publications

Praise for The Perfect Gentleman's Pocket Guide

"This book is a must-have for the modern man who wants to look perfectly polished, confident, and exude more charisma in business and social settings. This indispensable, easy-to-read guide gives you the tools to attract more joy, abundance, and even love in your life."

–Jacqueline Whitmore, Founder of The Protocol School of Palm Beach and author of POISED FOR SUCCESS

"Michael Ferrera could have written this book long ago! His sense of style and presence are unparalleled. It's one thing to dress well, but something else entirely to exemplify class and sophistication as a modern male. I put my best foot forward daily for millions of viewers to see. Michael Ferrera's new book will only enhance that effort!"

–Chris Schauble, Los Angeles TV News Anchor

"The Perfect Gentleman's Pocket Guide is an enjoyable and informative read! Michael's energetic charisma shines through all the pages of this book. It is a great read for both ladies and gentleman who value the characteristics of modern etiquette, manners and style."

–Alex O. Ellis, Founder of Tied To Greatness™ and author of RE-STORING THE MALE IMAGE

"There is no person that is perfect. Even a gentleman loses his mind on the occasion. What better way to get it back in order than The Perfect Gentleman's Pocket Guide? This book is to the point and accessible in any sticky situation."

–Enitan O. Bereola II, Author of BEREOLAESQUE: The Contemporary Gentleman & Etiquette Book For The Urban Sophisticate

"The Perfect Gentleman's Pocket Guide is a wonderful resource of valuable information for any person that wants an edge in the modern world of relationships, etiquette, and style."

—Jessica Matlock, Style Psychologist and President of Association of Image Consultants International Southern California

"After reading Michael Ferrera's Perfect Gentleman's Pocket Guide I concluded it is a must have, not just for every man that has a desire to be his personal best but every woman that has or desires a gentleman in her life should also have a copy of the guide. Having been fortunate enough to travel many regions of the world I thought I was in the know as it related to being the "perfect gentleman." After reading The PGPG I quickly realized I knew a lot less than I thought. PGPG is direct, and thorough beyond belief."

—Jon Covington, Founder of M.O.C.I.T.I. (Men of Color In The Industry)

"It is a pleasure to know and work with Michael Ferrera's radiant personality. Now as readers of his work, we hear his voice throughout these pages, a gentle persuasive sound that sets a wonderful tone in the book. I love the chapter titles and creative execution. It is easy to read and packed with valuable information. This is a brilliant book for every man in every situation."

—Jerri L. Rosen, CEO and Founder of Working Wardrobes

ISBN: 978-0-9853698-0-4 [Paperback]
ISBN: 978-0-9853698-1-1 [Hardcover]

Library of Congress Control Number: 2012905117

Cover Design by Brittany Fox
Illustrations by Clara J. Andres
Interior Design by TWA Solutions

Printed in the United States of America

M World Media Publications
915 Foothill Boulevard, Suite 362
Claremont, California 91711
books@michaelferrera.com
www.perfectgentlemanonline.com

This book is dedicated to my loving parents
Michael and Christine Ferrera

Words cannot express how grateful
I am for the both of you, so for now I will say:
Thank you

Preface

Imagine for a moment a man who is so pleasant to be in company with. His demeanor, character and charisma are as radiant as a summer day. He shakes hands with confidence; his smile and charm are as joyous as a young baby, while his style is as sharp as the Duke of Windsor on ball night. What if every gentleman you met embodied these characteristics? Imagine if every man walked and carried himself with such stature and integrity. Imagine that a woman would not be concerned about how a man would treat her because he embodied such grace. She would know that he would be dressed appropriately for any occasion. Imagine that from countless interactions, many thought that this gentleman was perfect. Now imagine if that gentleman was you.

It probably is. You simply have to display it!

Yours truly,

Michael Ferrera

Contents

Introduction

Welcome to The Perfect Gentleman's Pocket Guide. Within these pages you will find modern secrets to transforming and enhancing your mind and personality to be the perfect gentleman in life's most awkward situations. The PGPG, as I will refer to it, will not have a bunch of *fluff*, just answers and information that you can put to use immediately. You will not find a list of boring rules, to do's and not to do's or a ton of negative commentary about bad male habits. What you will find is insight as well as tools and tips that will enhance your manners, your style, and interactions throughout life. We have studied, referenced and researched countless etiquette books, style guides, and how-to-be-a-gentleman books so that you do not have to.

Based on extensive research, knowledge and experience, I've created The Perfect Gentleman's Pocket Guide for those moments in life when a quick reminder or insight could be very helpful to assist a gentleman with his manners or actions. Sure, you could read a 500-page etiquette book about which glass is yours or when to wear a tuxedo, but such a book is not always handy. The Perfect Gentleman's Pocket Guide is now that book. The PGPG has been designed to fit into most pockets—from briefcases, to pants, and suit coat pockets—for easy access and reference at the drop of a dime. It is a perfect tool for men to use and a refreshing resource for women. I encourage you to personalize it to your lifestyle, use it as you wish and share it to enhance the lives of other men and women. As we strive toward perfection as gentlemen, the journey can impact and empower several people along the way.

Let us embark upon the journey toward becoming the *Perfect Gentleman*.

How to Use This Book

All books are not designed to be read in the same manner. Some books are great and enjoyable when read once, while others are more powerful when read on multiple occasions. The PGPG is a book that lands at a hybrid. My recommendation is to read the whole book at least once, which will allow you to absorb foundational information regarding the characteristics of a perfect gentleman. Then, rather than reread the entire book, it is better to *revisit* and reference particular sections as needed. For example, in certain instances in life, simply turn through the pages of the PGPG for the section that applies, grab the information quickly, and be at your best in that situation. Another way to revisit this book is to carry it and have it handy for life's awkward moments. If you are heading to a fancy dinner or gala and you haven't been to such an event in a while, the PGPG is a nice point of reference on what you should wear, what silverware to use, or how to interact to avoid embarrassing situations. In addition, you will find my signature *Ferrera Fresh Tips* throughout the guide. They are simple, short, quick tips that are informational or add a bit more charisma to common scenarios. The *Ferrera Fresh*

Tips are yours to use and share with others for insightful and enjoyable conversations.

As a custom clothing designer and son of an etiquette professional, I have done my best to not be biased within these pages. I am a connoisseur of fine menswear and an aficionado of prestige manners. However, I do not feel that we all *need* custom clothes to look good or an etiquette coach to be well-behaved. With a little study and good company, we all can display grace and courtesy amongst the people with whom we interact. Therefore, use The Perfect Gentleman's Pocket Guide as it is appropriate to your lifestyle. Some things will apply to you and some may not. I challenge you to use the information that applies on a consistent basis so that we can enjoy one another throughout this beautiful gift we call life!

1

The Perfect Gentleman
Embodies Confidence

Rather than give you a list of rules that lead up to being a gentleman and conclude with a chapter on confidence, I will get right into it and say that the perfect gentleman always embodies confidence, period! Confidence is defined as the state of being certain that a chosen course of action is best or most effective by belief in oneself or abilities. In consideration of the formal definition, the perfect gentleman understands that confidence is one of the most important attributes a man embodies. In a small group or among large crowds, in a simple photo or under starlight, the perfect gentleman is confident in all aspects of life. The perfect gentleman's definition of self-confidence is the characteristic of a man is his abilities to perform and carry himself proudly with the respect of being considerate of others, even when there is the slightest doubt.

Why Confidence is Important

Confidence is important because it will cause other people to be confident in you. You being confident in yourself will cause others to feel confident in doing business with you, being associated with you, or going out with you on dates. When someone is interacting with you, they believe that there is something you offer that can bring value to the relationship, no matter how short or long the interaction. Therefore, being confident in your ability and skills will allow them to feel more comfortable with you. This applies to simple hangouts, social gatherings, business interactions and, of course, we know ladies embrace a confident man. Although the words will change with time such as "*your cool*," "*your flair*," "*your swagger*" or whatever else, they all mean confidence. The timid, "I don't know, I'm not sure" man will never be as effective as a respectful, confident gentleman.

Confident, Not Cocky

There is a difference between being confident and being cocky, and people can recognize the difference. The difference between a confident gentleman and a cocky man is that the cocky man *wants* attention while a confident gentleman *gets* attention without begging for it. Attention will naturally come to you, the perfect gentleman, because of your humility.

If you ever come in contact with a cocky person, never try to match or outdo their behavior. You can simply leave the environment or ignore them and carry on without being rude yourself. If you choose to address the issue at a later time, please do so. However, you may also choose not to interact with that person again. Regardless, never minimize your values as the perfect gentleman.

Ferrera Fresh Tip: There's no need to fake it 'til you make it! You already have confidence; you just have to believe you do and share it with everyone else you encounter.

Jealousy

As the perfect gentleman, it is inevitable that there will be other people who are envious, jealous, or trite toward you. We have come to know these people as "haters." These are the people who hate to see you succeed, hate your charm, your swagger, your kindness and charisma, for one reason or another. They may be disrespectful, dishonest, or rude among other things, but you cannot let that affect you. It comes with the territory of being the perfect gentleman. They want to be in your shoes and be around your kind, and since they are not, they don't want you to be either. Do not sweat it. Carry on as the perfect gentleman and teach others to enhance their lifestyle as well.

> *Ferrera Fresh Tip:* A gentleman compliments others and is never jealous! There is enough of everything for everyone on earth. Therefore, encourage others to continue in their success as you will continue to progress as well.

Keys to Building and Enhancing Confidence

♦ Enhancing your confidence begins in your mind. If you believe you can, then you will.

♦ When you are not sure, act out the task with confidence and be open to accepting a mistake. Your confidence and positive attitude to take action may even cause the minor error to be overlooked.

♦ Confidence does not mean being cocky. There is never a need for a gentleman to rudely boast or brag about anything.

◆ Although others may think you're cocky at times, do not let it bother you. Carry on as the perfect gentleman.

◆ Practice confidence. Practice being comfortable with being uncomfortable. Practice taking confident *actions* when you are not completely confident. This will allow you to accept mistakes and be unafraid to make them. It might sound scary at first, but it works!

> *Ferrera Fresh Tip:* Confidence is one of the most important characteristics of the perfect gentleman. Beyond clothes, money, and above all else, confidence screams volumes without saying anything. Display it.

As we embark upon this journey of becoming and enhancing the perfect gentleman, there will not be a list of rules to do and not to do. However, there is one "rule" you must know, even if you remember or use nothing else from this book. That rule is to embrace confidence! This characteristic alone will get you farther in any situation I will guide you through within these pages. There will even be times when your actions are confident while you are not so confident in your mind. At this point, you have reached one of the highest levels of a gentleman's confidence. It is where you are comfortable with being uncomfortable. It takes practice. But with class and the willingness to learn, the perfect gentleman will be able to handle any situation in life when displaying humble confidence.

2
The Perfect Gentleman
Is Groomed Inside and Out

Please know that the characteristics of a gentleman are displayed long before anyone else even sees you. It is a way of life, a variety of characteristics that exude excellence from the moment you arise. The key to grooming, as the perfect gentleman, is understanding the essence of *time*. Whether brief or long, allow yourself enough time to do all the things that are essential to grooming yourself for the day or event. If it is a day when you need to shave, you may want to allot a bit more time to get the perfect shave. If you need to polish your shoes, allow enough time for your shoes to get a nice shine. These things will create huge benefits throughout the day. The reason this is so important is that the five to ten minutes of tardiness while grooming can have a domino effect on the rest of your day. It could cause you to be late for a meeting, a date, or another event, which is completely unacceptable as the perfect gentleman. If you are not sure about general hygiene or tasks required, there are other books that you may need to reference in addition to this one. This section of The Perfect Gentleman's Pocket

Guide will be brief, but it is absolutely necessary to understand these aspects of health and hygiene while carrying on as the perfect gentleman.

Brushing

Brushing teeth is one of the beginning and most important aspects of good hygiene. Naturally, your mouth is the area of your body that carries the most germs, so it is important to keep your mouth clean and fresh. A few notes the perfect gentleman knows about mouth care are:

- A good mouthwash is great to have. Used after brushing, it leaves a fresh scent in your mouth. Another benefit is mouthwash kills bacterial germs that cause bad breath.
- Flossing is another component of mouth care that allows for fresh breath. Floss every opportunity you have prior to brushing to clean between teeth and then brush the teeth clean after flossing.
- Throughout the day, a rinse with mouthwash can be very helpful specifically after meals or before a meeting. You may want to keep a small bottle of mouthwash with you in your office desk drawer for random refreshing as needed.
- A thorough brushing can be completed in two to three minutes. Keep it short, but keep it clean!

Ferrera Fresh Tip: The roof and the tongue are parts of the mouth; remember to brush them!

Bathing

I do not know what's worst—bad breath or bad body odor. Regardless of which, the perfect gentleman does both and does them well. Gents, please know that it is okay to take a shower or bath more than once a day. Yes, we may want to relax in the house all day on the weekends or on days off, but you can still be fresh! When cleaning the body, the perfect gentleman knows:

♦ Showers do not have to be long. Five to ten minutes is enough time to cleanse the body well.

♦ Prior to entering the shower, run the water for about 30 seconds to rid minor bacteria in the showerhead, which is common. However, a gentleman knows the bathroom should have a thorough cleaning at least once a week.

♦ Try shampooing your hair first so that any remaining suds can be washed away when rinsing off after washing the body.

♦ A loofah or soap sponge holds less germs than a washcloth, but choose what you like. If you use a wash-cloth, change it every one to two days. If you use a loofah, change it every 30-45 days to make sure you are cleaning the body with fresh and clean items, which only makes sense.

♦ When finished bathing, there should be no sign you were there other than a few water drops. Make sure all hair and soapsuds are washed away before exiting. There should also be no clothes or towels left behind on the floor. You're the perfect gentleman.

- When done, remember to dry your whole body before putting on your clothes. I know we all get lazy or in a rush at times, but avoid putting clothes on a wet body, which is simply inappropriate.

Lotion and Powder

- You are not a woman, but lotion (especially lotion designed for men) is meant to add essential vitamins to our bodies and to keep skin healthy. Use it!

- You may want to consider investing in a face lotion and body lotion, which can be a bit different. Face lotion will be gentler and more beneficial to your face as that is what it is designed for. Nonetheless, your regular lotion will work for your face as well. Just remember to use lotion.

- Powder is a great way to stay fresh and keep dry. You may want to consider using it in private areas.

- Very little powder is needed, and remember to put it on before your clothes so that powder is not on your clothes.

Washing Your Face

As the perfect gentleman, you should wash your face at minimum once a day. The best time to rid your face of excess oil and dirt is at the end of the day, before bed. Then perform a light wash in the morn when you arise. When choosing your face wash, some type of male exfoliating wash is best to open your pores to eliminate any blackheads or pimples. However, avoid using an exfoliating face wash every day since it can scratch and damage the skin if used too often. Using an exfoliating face wash two to three times a week will be enough to keep skin healthy. In between your exfoliating face wash, or alternating days, opt for a smooth face wash to keep your skin clean. When choosing a face wash you may have to try a few options or ask a professional for recommendations. I know we are not women, but we still need to care for our faces to some extent. As the perfect gentleman:

- Remember to also apply the facial wash under your chin and neck. This will be beneficial when shaving, which we will talk about in the shaving section.

- Contrary to what is best for women, as a man you can wash your face in the shower, which also saves time.

- Let the facial wash sit on your face for about 20 seconds to allow the exfoliating materials to work or use as directed on the product.

- Begin washing your face with warm water (which opens your pores) and rinse your face with slightly cooler water to close your pores.

- When finished, *set* your face into the towel multiple times to dry. Do not wipe your face with the towel too hard, as if you are finishing a shower. This can be harmful to the skin on your freshly cleaned face.

> *Ferrera Fresh Tip:* It is perfectly fine for a gentleman to treat himself to a professional facial every now and again. It is also a great way to gain professional information on daily care for your individual face.

Shaving

Unless you are going for the rugged caveman look, or just rather not shave, a clean shave is always appropriate for the perfect gentleman. That is not to say there is anything wrong with having a beard. Some gentleman can look better with a beard, just as a smooth face works better for other gents. Shaving is an art, and there are certain professionals that can groom your beard and mustache in a manner that simply cannot be done through regular day-to-day shaving. Using a razor or electric shaver from day to day is completely up to you. Try both options at different times and decide what you personally prefer. Consider things like, if it's easy to use, how often you want to shave, and your look and comfort, of course. If you have the time and money, I would recommend getting a professional shave at least once a month to keep your facial hair growing properly and to gain professional advice on how to take care of your facial hair regularly. For day-to-day shaving, the perfect gentleman knows:

- Always use a clean and sharp razor in either wet or dry shaving methods.

- If doing some type of design in your beard or side burns, be confident and go for it. Hesitation may cause you to make mistakes.

- Shave along the grain, or the direction in which your facial hair grows. The hair on your neck often grows *up* in the opposite direction of your other facial hair.

- Shaving in the correct direction will cause less razor irritation, allowing you a more comfortable feeling when you are done shaving.

- It is best to go against the hair grain only when your hair is already low and you're finishing up for a very close shave.

- It is important to note that hair closer to your lower neck may grow up in the opposite direction and it is important to shave that way to minimize irritation.

Razor Shave

- A razor shave or wet shave is arguably the closest shave you can get for regular day-to-day shaving.

- It is often better to shave after you shower rather than before. After a shower your skin is clean and warm, which are means for a better, closer shave.

- The key to a great razor shave is moisture. Create or use a great shaving cream that does not dry fast. It is important to keep your face moist in order to minimize any nicks or cuts.

- If the phone rings or if some unimportant interruption happens while shaving, ignore it. You do not want your face to get dry by taking a break.

- You may need to shave more often to keep a clean look. Since your hair is already close to your face, it may grow faster.

- Make sure all the shaving cream is gone from your face when finished.

Electric Shave

* You should use some type of pre-shave or electric shaving powder, which allows the razor to glide smoother over your face.

* Often unknown but important with electric dry shaving is that you do not *have* to wash your face prior to shaving. This is because you want your facial hair to be as dry as possible, allowing your hair to stand up in preparation for a closer shave.

* To give an even finish, especially if you are going for a bearded look, try brushing or combing your facial hair before, during and after you shave.

* If using an electric shave method, it is better to wash your face normally with a smooth face cleanser when you are finished, and *then apply* your aftershave.

Ferrera Fresh Tip: When learning to shave, humbly ask someone to teach you. You will feel more comfortable as you continue to practice and you will avoid unnecessary cuts, nicks and scratches.

Aftershave

Good facial care involves aftershave and yes you can deal with the light sting. Suck it up, gent. But a few things to remember as the perfect gentleman are:

* Use aftershave immediately after a wet shave, but use it after you wash your face when dry shaving. Apply it to all areas of your face you shaved or edged up.

* Aftershaves can come in lotions, liquids, creams as well as other forms. Among the options, find something you like and make sure it works.

◆ Working means that it leaves a cool feeling, it feels good when it is applied, it does not sting too much, and it eliminates razor bumps or irritation.

◆ You may need to try a few aftershaves before you find the one that you like and that works for you.

◆ Get aftershave recommendations from your barber or professional. Try them and make your own informed decisions.

◆ I recommend opting for an aftershave lotion rather than a liquid. Lotion moisturizes your face while liquid often dries it. Lotion is my recommendation, but always choose what is comfortable to you.

> *Ferrera Fresh Tip:* A great site for shaving tips and ideas is www.TheMensroom.com by Craig The Barber. Take a look when you have a chance. I am sure you will be pleased!

Ingrown Hairs

Ingrown facial hair happens when facial hair begins to grow, but does not penetrate your skin. Rather, it grows *into* your skin. It can be very irritating and can be very painful. As the perfect gentleman, you must know how to handle this should the situation occur. Ingrown hair can occur with either wet or dry shaving methods, but occurs more often when using a wet razor shave because the hair is cut very low or even cut to be under the skin already. It is also more common for gents that have curly hair, so be mindful. A few tips the perfect gentleman knows to avoid and take care of ingrown hairs are:

- Clean your face well and regularly. Often ingrown hair is the result of dirt, oil and natural buildup on your face that can cause hair to grow incorrectly.

- Care for your face. Examine your face every now and again to see if any ingrown hair is starting. Do not do this in public but rather in your own private space.

- Shave often. If you're going for a beard, comb or brush it daily so that your hair grows correctly.

- If ingrown hair starts to grow into your skin, try washing your face with your exfoliating face wash first to see if it will release the hair from your skin.

- If that does not work, simply grab a clean pair of tweezers and move the hair so that the tip is no longer in your skin, allowing it to grow normal. You do not need to pull the hair out of the root, just out from under your skin.

- If the ingrown hair has already formed, you have a bit more work to do. Grab the tweezers again, but now you may have to break or open the skin slightly where the hair has grown, allowing it to come out from under your skin.

- Finally, you may want to add a small amount of ointment on the area you have just plucked so that it heals properly. A good facial lotion is not a bad idea either.

Ferrera Fresh Tip: Your girlfriend or spouse can help you with those uncomfortable ingrown hairs you cannot see. She is also more familiar with using tweezers than you are, so have her help you.

Haircuts, Hairstyle and Hair Care

Pick a style and stick to it for a while. Contrary to popular opinion, you can do the cool mini Mohawk, streaks or even choose color. Times have changed, but the etiquette on keeping your hair neat and in order has not! Keep it clean, professional and stylish. In regards to hair styling and care, the perfect gentleman knows:

♦ A separate shampoo and conditioner is best for any type of hair, especially if your hair is longer than one inch. But a 2-in-1 shampoo and conditioner works fine as well.

♦ Hair does not need to be washed every day. Washing your hair every two to three days is enough for your body to replenish its natural elements.

♦ If you have a full beard, you can use shampoo and conditioner on your facial hair as you use it on your head of hair. And yes, you can use both for hair on private areas as well. It's still hair that needs to be clean and healthy.

♦ The period between your haircuts is dependent on the gent, but often a once-a-week trim, edge up or full cut will keep a gentleman sharp.

♦ Remember to trim sideburns, nose and ears hair regularly with every cut. It looks neater, so ask your barber or do it yourself.

♦ You may need to trim eyebrow hair as well, but ditch any fancy eyebrow designs or fancy grooming. A clean but natural look is more mature.

♦ In between cuts, brush or comb your hair as needed. Once or twice a day will do.

◆ After brushing, do a check that no hair or particles are remaining on your clothes, especially if wearing black. Dust off your shoulders as needed.

◆ Understand your profession when styling your hair. Regardless of how cool you are, you always want to be professional with your hairstyle. In some cases, you may want to ditch the fancy patterns or styles.

◆ Do not brush your hair in public. No matter how fancy your hair is, no one needs to see you grooming yourself. If you really *need* to, go to the men's room, your car or a private place.

I promise, ladies love a regularly well-groomed man, and they will appreciate your "After 5" shadow at times, too! Finally, be real with yourself. The perfect gentleman knows which hairstyle is appropriate for his profession. If not, ask someone or another respected professional.

Ferrera Fresh Tip: Build a relationship with your barber and respect his or her time. A good relationship will help when you need random favors or a rush cut.

Pubic Shaving

As a gentleman, please know that pubic hair shaving is completely up to you. You can choose to "tame the mane" or go natural. You do not *have* to ask the lady you are with about her preference. Choose for yourself. You can ask for her opinion, but personally choose what option you like best. Either way, remember to keep your pubic hair neat as mentioned in hair care. If you chose to shave, the perfect gentleman knows:

- First and foremost, be careful! You laugh, but we both know this is an important area.
- Treat and prepare for this shave as you would with shaving the hair on your face. Use either wet or dry shaving methods as stated above.
- If you choose to razor shave, this can be done in the shower and there is very little cleanup. Just the opposite, dry trimming is easy, but there is a bit more cleanup you will need to do.
- Use a comb that is dedicated only for this area. Move hair away from your body as you trim to your desired length and trim to your liking.
- All other shaving tips apply as well, but there is no need for aftershave in this area. The best option is to simply shower normally when you are finished.

Ferrera Fresh Tip: Choices on pubic grooming, underarm, or leg shaving are completely personal preference and there is nothing wrong with shaving them. Whichever your choice, choose with confidence!

Cologne

One of the perfect gentleman's finishing touches is his cologne. However, it is important to note that cologne is not always *needed*. A fresh shower, deodorant, and lotion can make for a great natural-smelling gent. One thing ladies will always remember is the scent of a man, even long after he is gone. So if you want to stay on her mind, smell good. When using cologne, the perfect gentleman knows:

- There is no need to use a lot of cologne. One or two touches or sprays on the neck and wrist are enough.

- Get rid of the five to ten sprays. If you can smell your own cologne on yourself unintentionally, you are wearing too much.

- Use cologne after the shower, not after you're dressed. Your pores are open and skin is damp so it will last longer throughout the day or event.

- If you forget, yes, you can use it once dressed. But try to put it on your skin, not on your clothes.

- "How do you take some cologne off if you have too much on despite my earlier warnings?" It's tough to do, but normal hand and face rinsing will probably help.

- Try not to use cologne to cover up a bad odor. I guess it's better than nothing, but it can make for a mixed, awkward smell.

- Try not to "save" your cologne because you do not want to use it up too fast. Cologne loses its strength, color and scent if it just sits around too long. So use it and replace it when finished.

Ferrera Fresh Tip: Find a cologne set with matching aftershave, soap, and deodorant that you like. It gives off an even bodily smell and it allows you to use less cologne. Ladies will love this, gents.

Finger & Toe Nails

The most important thing is to keep them clean! Whether you choose longer nails or short nails, keep them clean. I definitely recommend short because they are easier to care for with low maintenance.

- After cutting your finger or toenails, wash your hands or feet, which will make for a nice clean look when you are done. And, remember to lotion when finished.

- Whether you are an athlete, business professional or a beach boy, clean cut toenails will allow your feet to feel more comfortable in your shoes.

- There is nothing wrong with a gentleman having a manicure or pedicure occasionally. In fact, it is better for your hands and feet to have professional care regularly. But, of course, no nail polish, not even clear polish.

- I know you do not want to go into the same place your girlfriend or spouse goes for a manicure. So search for a men's spa that may offer the service along with massages, facials and all the trimmings. It is not girly, and you will probably appreciate it!

> *Ferrera Fresh Tip*: Visit a relaxation spa periodically, gentlemen. It releases stress and is healthy for your body. But don't get carried away; you're still a man!

Manners and Hygiene

Coughing and Sneezing

If you have to cough or sneeze in public, do your best to keep in your range. If your handkerchief is not handy, sneeze or cough into your left shoulder or armpit area since there is not much interaction with others there. Covering your mouth or nose with your *left* hand is fine too; just wash your hands when you have a chance. There is no need for obnoxious outbursts or sneezing everywhere, coughing without covering your mouth or clearing mucous from your throat in front

Ferrera Fresh Tip: Remember, if a person around you coughs or sneezes in the open, do not turn up your face with disgust. If it is continuous and obnoxious, you can move or politely ask them to cover their mouth.

of people. Yes, that is nasty! Go to the restroom and take care of yourself. If your cough or sneeze is bad and you are not near a restroom, simply step away for a quick moment.

Spitting

Spitting was probably one of the coolest things to do as a young boy, but as the perfect gentleman, spitting is not always appropriate. On the sports field, feel free to spit. Know how and where to spit on the field. But in public, do not do it. Simply head to the restroom and spit in the toilet, then flush.

Ferrera Fresh Tip: If you simply have to spit, just be as respectful as possible to others. It's not that pleasant to anyone.

If you are in public and you really have to spit, try to spit on a grass or dirt area, where there may not be a lot of walking traffic, or use a tissue and throw it away immediately.

Burping

Another so-called "cool thing" to do as a young boy is not as appropriate as the perfect gentleman. The key to burping is controlling it. The loud boisterous outburst is completely uncalled for, even in a room full of other men. If you are alone in your own home, loud burping is still a maybe, but you have more freedom. Regardless, every time you burp, say "Excuse me" and carry on, even when you have an awkward, unexpected burp. I suggest saying, "Excuse me" when you are alone so you can create a habit of always doing it. Finally, try to burp with your mouth closed and cover your mouth. This is a great way

Ferrera Fresh Tip: In addition to burping, always remember to cover your mouth when you yawn. It's just not a good look and can be taken as rude by others.

to *control* your burp and avoid disturbing others or being rude in public.

Flatulence

Flatulence is the formal word for passing gas or fart. It would be a lot easier to not talk about this in the PGPG, but the perfect gentleman must know how to handle it since it will come up in life. The best thing to do is to leave to the restroom, handle your business and return. Yes, I know you can't keep going to the restroom every time, so hold it every now and again. Then, when you head for a regular bathroom break, go ahead and *break wind*. If it does happen by accident in a large group, casually leave the area and you may want to make your way outside, hoping a smell does not linger. If you cannot leave, just hope it is not too bad of a smell and act normal. No apology is needed unless it is clearly known that it is you. If someone else around you passes gas, do not embarrass the person by making a rude comment. Unfortunately, you should just bear with it for a moment and carry on.

Sick

The perfect gentleman is not a perfect human and does get sick at times. If that is the case, minimize all interaction with other people as much as possible. Do your best to chill, relax and get better. Simple medication with rest, rest, and more rest is probably the best remedy. If the problem persists, visit a professional physician for assistance. If you have to attend or cannot miss an appointment while sick, the perfect gentleman knows:

• Do your best not to *look* sick. Walk, talk, dress and act as normal as possible. You have decided to go to your appointments, so be at your best as possible. You might even beat the sickness by not giving in to it.

• Minimize shaking hands. Simply say, "I'm just getting over a sickness…" and motion as to tip your hat as a form of greeting.

• Some shaking of hands may have to occur, so keep your handkerchief or tissue handy. You should also have a small hand sanitizer close by to kill germs.

• Try not to stay too close to others for long periods, especially in small, closed area.

• Before a meeting it is okay to share briefly that you are a little sick and try to shorten the appointment or interaction and resume when you are better. This will be more beneficial to everyone.

Ferrera Fresh Tip: When you cough or sneeze, you should use your left hand or left shoulder as much as possible. You will most likely shake with the right hand and this will minimize germs.

Health, Nutrition and Fitness

First off, the PGPG is not your nutritional guide to success, but I will share with you a few ideas that can be a quick reference of helpful hints on health, nutrition and fitness.

As part of being a gentleman, being healthy on the inside is just as or even more important as being well groomed and well dressed. Besides, without good health, we are not as effective as we can be. In keeping a balanced diet, the perfect gentleman knows:

- What should and should not be eaten *often*. Even junk food has a benefit to the body, even if it is simply for personal enjoyment every once in a while.

- We all know vegetables, brown rice and oatmeal are not the most exciting things to eat, but you may want to eat some boring foods because of the health benefits they can bring to your body.

- Some vegetables that are particularly great for men are: broccoli, cabbage, squash, romaine lettuce and tomatoes, to name a few. Make sure to add these into your diet regularly.

- Eating more than three times a day is not always bad. Eating more often in smaller quantities can be healthier to your body by causing your metabolism to speed up. Your metabolism increases as your muscles are constantly working to digest food and burn fat. This is best with an active and busy lifestyle.

- Water is simply one of the earth's best resources. Although it can be boring to drink, make sure you get enough.

- Unfortunately, there is not any cookie cutter "drink this much water a day" fact for every man. Because we are all different, it is best to consult your personal doctor and use common sense, making sure you are not thirsty.

♦ When the body is more active, drink all natural juices and occasional sports drinks. Although they may have a lot of sugar, they also have electrolytes and vitamins that can replenish the nutrients your body loses from activity.

♦ Minimize beverages with high fructose corn syrup, which is a man-made, chemical-based sugar that can make anything taste good. Your body technically does not recognize how to digest it, which is not good for the body.

♦ The key is to minimize high fructose corn syrup because it can be hard to eliminate while keeping a balanced diet.

A Gentleman's Minimum Daily Fruits and Vegetables

Gentleman Age 16-30	Fruits	Vegetables
Less Active	2 cups	3 cups
Active	2 ½ cups	4 cups

Gentleman Age 31-50	Fruits	Vegetables
Less Active	2 cups	3 cups
Active	2 ½ cups	3 ½ cups

Gentleman Age 51+	Fruits	Vegetables
Less Active	2 cups	2 ½ cups
Active	2 cups	3 cups

Fitness

When working out in private or at a fitness center, remember that your manners as the perfect gentleman and all communication skills fully apply, which you will read more about later in the communication chapter. Just because your muscles are showing, does not give way to being inconsiderate of those around you. If you do work out in private and alone, it is good to let someone know that you will be working out. In case of any emergency, they'll know where you are.

Regardless of where you work out, the perfect gentleman knows:

* Fitness professionals have confirmed that it is healthy for a male to exercise a minimum of 30 minutes a day for three to four days a week. Be creative. This can be done even with an extremely busy schedule.

* When in the fitness center, be respectful to the space of others and the location as a whole. Try not to cough, spit, or sneeze in areas designated for everyone's use. Carrying a personal towel is great to minimize germs.

* Try to clean up your sweat after you use a station and let others use areas you are not using.

* Say hello, nod or engage in small conversations, but never interrupt anyone's workout.

* If someone is interrupting you, simply chat for a second and say, "Please let me get back to my workout. Maybe we can talk in a minute" and move on. No heavy explanation needed.

- Spot weights and help others if they ask, and never be embarrassed to ask for help yourself. You will look more foolish if you get hurt.

- Ditch the unnecessary grunts and "I'm-pushing-a-lot-of-weight" noises to attract attention in the gym. If heavy breathing occurs naturally, that is fine. But there is no need to exaggerate and don't forget to breathe. Ladies will naturally notice you as the perfect gentleman.

Ferrera Fresh Tip: Get your workout in regularly. Not only is it healthy, but ladies love it too.

Fitness & Females

In regards to ladies at the gym, remember to stay focused on your workout! Yes, I know it is difficult not to look at the sexy, sweaty ladies with minimal clothes on in the gym, but the perfect gentleman knows:

- Respectfully look, but DO NOT STARE! Ladies know when you are looking and some appreciate a glance, but ladies also know when you are gawking. Most of them hate it, so don't do it.

- If you are attracted to someone simply say hello every so often and let her initiate more of the conversation.

- Even in short conversations, do not fully dive in by asking for phone numbers. It is better to just feel the vibe and take signs from the conversation. Some ladies are just being nice, but some are interested.

- If you do feel like you want to pursue a conversation, use all the Ferrera Fresh Tips discussed later in this book and make it happen.

♦ Commenting on her good gym work ethic and discipline, if you see her often, can be a great way to get a quick smile and start a conversation. Just be genuine in your conversation.

♦ Do not try to hit on her by saying she is using the exercise equipment wrong! Yes, help her only if she asks or after you get to know her, but it is not a good way to flirt in the gym.

♦ Whistling, screaming and hollering at a lady in an attempt to talk to her at the gym is not a good idea either. The gym is simply another environment to be a gentleman. Approach a lady respectfully as in any other setting.

> *Ferrera Fresh Tip:* Yes, you will see the sexy ladies at the gym when you're with other guys, but keep your cool when you tell your friend to "look at her!" Remember, glance; don't stare.

As the perfect gentleman in regards to your health, hygiene and grooming, it is important to remember that being the perfect gentleman begins far before anyone sees you. It is a mindset, a lifestyle, characteristics and charm in you that will allow you to be embraced by others. Hygiene and health may not be characteristics that people can actually see, but they are important in your overall presentation as the perfect gentlemen. As you prepare and groom as the perfect gentleman be cognizant of the time you need to complete your grooming tasks and plan accordingly. You will not need hours of time to get prepared once being clean and well-groomed becomes a habit for you. Then you can explore the options of fashion and style that will complete your look as the perfect gentleman.

3
The Perfect Gentleman
Understands Style

t is often said that clothes make the man. I beg to differ and suggest that clothes do not make the man but *enhance* the man. That is to say, appearance and style are important, but they should not define you. A gentleman does not chase trends as they will come and go, but a neat and clean appearance is always in style. As a custom clothier and stylist, I do believe that a gentleman can be very well dressed, and appropriately so without necessarily having custom clothes. However, I do highly recommend every man experience custom or bespoke clothes when you are ready to take your image to a more personalized look. The comfort, style, feel, and options available with custom clothing are simply unmatched by any items you will find off-the-rack, and of course www.michaelferrera.com is a great place for your custom clothing needs. Regardless of which option you choose, the secret behind the attire of a gentleman is the *confidence* he embodies when dressed. Therefore, I encourage you to be confident in whatever you are wearing because your confidence will show and will say much more than your clothing alone.

Embrace your inner style!

Hopefully, you understand that items such as underwear, T-shirts, shorts, socks, and sneakers are basic necessities in a gentleman's wardrobe. Therefore, I will not go into too much detail about them. In addition to those items, there are some things the perfect gentleman must have in his wardrobe at all times, ready and available. I will begin this style chapter with a list of the top ten items the perfect gentleman should own. These items are also a great way to start building a wonderful wardrobe.

> *Ferrera Fresh Tip:* You do not "need" custom clothes to look good in your style, but there is a difference. When you are ready, treat yourself. You are worth it!

10 Things in the Perfect Gentleman's Wardrobe

1. A Dark Suit

As the perfect gentleman, you should own at least one suit, even if you only wear it a few times a year. A two-piece suit in either black or blue is a must for any gentleman's wardrobe. If you can find a three-piece suit, get it because it will pay off handsomely in the future. I recommend choosing a dark blue suit because it is more versatile. A dark two-piece can be used as a full business suit, casual as a coat with khakis, or minus the tie it can create what I call the "corporate cool" look when going to dinner and social events. Sometimes, it can also be pulled off as formal wear with a crisp white shirt, cuff links, and a bowtie.

2.   White or Blue Dress Shirt

The white or blue shirt is classic, and if you are able to get both as you start your wardrobe, please do. Then add a variety of other colors, patterns and stripes as you build your wardrobe. White or blue are best when starting a wardrobe because of the versatility. These colors are perfect for the business world and can easily be dressed down by ditching the tie and going with the top one or two buttons undone. As you enhance your wardrobe, I encourage you to be adventurous with variations of yellows, hues of blue and even salmon pink. Feel free to consider stripes, checks and even floral patterns. Learn what you like and dislike, as this is how you will define your style.

3.   Dark Leather Dress Shoes

The third piece the perfect gentleman should own is a pair of black leather dress shoes. Some stylish gentlemen may consider black shoes to be boring; however, black shoes are universal and serve a purpose. Opt for a thinner leather sole shoe rather than a thick rubber sole. The leather-soled shoes will last longer and look a bit more mature. A rubber sole shoe is appropriate at times as well but can sometimes look a bit clunky, which is not the most stylish option for the perfect gentleman in you. You may need to invest a little more money in leather shoes, but it will be well worth it. Once you have the basic black, expand your wardrobe by adding brown leather, suede shoes, and even burgundy leather to add a little flair and style, other than the norm, which are absolutely perfect for the perfect gentleman.

4. Dark Leather Belt

A normal men's stylebook would say that your belt should always match your shoes. This will always be a classic and always appropriate. However, as your wardrobe evolves you may consider matching your belt with your tie or socks for style. A black belt to match your black shoes might be your first choice, but also consider getting a reversible belt as your first option when starting your wardrobe. This will give you a black belt and by flipping the buckle, it will provide you with a brown belt you can wear with your brown shoes as well. Try to choose a belt with a silver buckle, which is more subtle than gold when you are wearing it often. After you have your basic belts, you can explore other colors, fabrics, and textures to enhance your style.

5. Jeans

Denim is the new century casual pants for men since the fabric can be comfortable and cool. Denim, because of its toughness, was initially only worn by rigorous workers such as cowboys or steel engineers and they often wore one classic blue color. Oh how denim has evolved. When starting a wardrobe, it is better to have darker blue denim, which can be worn in casual settings or for dressier occasions with a collared shirt and blazer. Remember, the darker the denim, the dressier it will look and the lighter the denim, the more casual it will look. Keep in mind that jeans are simply another style of pants, which means you can have them tailored as you would your slacks. There is no need to have the back of your jeans cuff torn and sloppy because they are too long. A tailor shop or cleaners can take care of this for you. When you invest in a good pair of jeans, it is quite possible for them to last a very long time, so choose wisely.

6. Khaki Pants

Khaki pants can be a nice enhancement to your wardrobe. This piece of garment can be worn at business casual events or social events. You can wear this item with your dress shirts, polo shirts, and blazers, which is why it is so useful. Add your dark shoes and belt with this piece, and you are set. Opt for a light brown or beige color for starters; then add navy blue, black, and olive colors with time. In addition, corduroy is a fabric that is often overlooked but is a very cool option that can replace or be added to your chino pants collection.

7. Polo Shirts

Polo shirts in the wardrobe are the most versatile pieces of clothing because they never go out of style or season. I highly recommend having a wide variety of them! With denim, slacks or chino pants, polo shirts make for a very classy look. It is great to have your favorite colors and also colors that accent your facial features. If you have the Frank Sinatra baby blue eyes, try different hues of blues and pastels. For the brown-eyed gentleman, try rust, orange or variations of browns. When choosing your polo shirt colors, any color can be worn as long as you wear it with confidence. Just like any other clothing item, make sure your polos fit. Know your personal chest, shoulder and collar measurements and shop accordingly.

Ferrera Fresh Tip: For style, remember to pair colors you wear with the seasons. Ladies love a man who knows how and when to wear certain colors.

8. Dark Color Socks

The only man that could get away with white athletic socks and dress shoes was the late Michael Jackson, so don't try it. Commonly, your socks should match your pants for a smooth transition into pairing with your shoes. When buying socks, they may come in bundles. Blue, black and brown are fine, but remember to add more of the same colors in different patterns and designs. Contrary to the norm, I do believe you can have fun with your socks. If you like argyles, wild colors, or awkward fun socks, go for it! Life is too short, so have fun with this part of your wardrobe. Just remember, there is a thin line between having cool socks

Ferrera Fresh Tip: Do not wear white gym socks with your dress shoes! If you only have one pair of dark dress socks, wash them after every use and wear them again.

and socks that are flat out ridiculous. Just take note on how comfortable you are when others respond and you decide.

9. Ties

It is hard to suggest one color, but for starters, grab a colorful type of blue. There can be other colors in the tie and a unique design that can make your tie versatile. This will make the tie perfect for your suit and still give you a little uniqueness rather than just the politician blue suit, white shirt and red tie look. Add yellow, pink, orange, or purple ties if you choose as well. Some men are afraid to experiment with colors other than the three three main tie colors, but color is what will attract people to you, so use it! The trick with your neckwear in the beginning is to find ties with multiple colors already in the pattern that looks good together and matches well with your shirts and suits. Once you are confident with those styles and colors, mix and match, which will allow you to further enhance your style.

10. Pocket Squares

The pocket square is a piece that is often forgotten, but the perfect gentleman will learn to appreciate it. When choosing your pocket square, you can almost never go wrong with a nice cotton or silk white. As your collection grows, different colors and patterns are all wonderful. Please know that you do not have to match your pocket square in the exact pattern as your tie. In fact, it is better not to match your tie and pocket square exactly. It looks too "cookie cutter," as if you have no style of your own. Contrary to popular opinion, you can mix and match patterns in your pocket square with other patterns you are wearing. It is a bold look, but it looks great.

> *Ferrera Fresh Tip*: Don't forget to add bowties to your tie collection! A bowtie is a nice escape from the norm, but everyone can't pull it off.

Now that you know the essentials, this section of the PGPG is categorized for quick references on each clothing item. You will find the section header of the clothing item and then you will see a few important points regarding the item, such as the right fit, how to wear it, style tips, plus clean and care. This will be your guide to shopping and enhancing your styles. You will also find a chart titled the Perfect Gentleman's Dress Code, which you can reference for when you should wear what, such as at a black tie or white tie event. Finally, in this section you will continue to see the Ferrera Fresh Tips for you to remember and use as you wish!

> *Ferrera Fresh Tip*: Get an additional handkerchief to serve as the one you use because the one in the front chest pocket is simply for style!

SUITS

The suit, or the "international business uniform," as I call it, should always be ready and available for the perfect gentleman. The reason I call it the international business uniform is that anywhere you go on the globe, men wear two-piece business suits at one time or another, which cannot be said about any other garment. From the United Nations meeting to a simple dinner with your wife, a good suit is a necessity. Let us begin with looking at the parts of the suit individually in order to enhance your understanding of style.

The Suit Jacket

Fit

A well-fitting suit is the most important aspect, even above color and style. Find a good tailor and build a relationship with him so he will know your body and style. The only thing worse than a badly tailored suit is not having one.

- To begin your jacket fit, make sure the jacket lands comfortably on your shoulders. The seams from the shoulder to the sleeves should meet exactly where your shoulder and arm join on your body.

- The suit sleeve width should wrap around your biceps and forearm comfortably to your liking.

- The suit sleeve length should land approximately one quarter or one-half inch above your wrist line where your wrist and forearm join when your hands are at your side. This will allow for your shirt sleeves to fall at your wrist for a perfect finishing image when your jacket is on.

- The length of your coat should land in the middle of your hand when your hands are at your side while your coat is on.

Ferrera Fresh Tip: When traveling with a suit that has flap front pockets, wear the flaps out one day and tucked in on another day. You will give a different image with the same suit, plus you'll minimize the number of suits you need to carry.

Style

Double Breasted

The double-breasted suit jacket originates from the ancient and military era. It has a very classic military look that will be worn by men for a long time. Although this is an older style of suit jacket, it has been widely modernized by having more buttons for style. A few things to remember when choosing a double-breasted suit are:

- The term double-breasted is used because the left front of the jacket *doubles* over the right side of the jacket and over the chest or *breast* of the body.

- There are buttons on the inside of the left jacket front that should always be used so the jacket looks neat when it is buttoned.

- When you hear the term *four on two*, this means that the front of the double-breasted jacket has four buttons above a pair of buttons that are meant to be used.

- Additional buttons on the front of a double-breasted

jacket make for a more modern look and feel. Just don't overdo it on the number of buttons on your suit.

- When wearing a double-breasted jacket while standing, you should always wear it buttoned to keep the form of the jacket. When you sit down, you can unbutton it.

Single Breasted

The single breasted is a more popular and modern style suit jacket. It is very versatile and it looks good as a full suit or mixed and matched with your slacks and even jeans. This is a great option to choose for your first suit. A few things to remember regarding the single-breasted suit jacket are:

- It is more modern and convenient since it is more versatile in the wardrobe.

- Always keep the bottom button of your single-breasted jacket undone. This allows you to have easier access to your pants pockets when your jacket is on. Also, it prevents you from looking like an uptight mannequin.

- A three-button jacket is the classic business option and is a good choice.

- The two-button, single-breasted jacket gives a more stylish look, allowing more of your shirt and tie to be seen when your jacket is buttoned.

Pockets

Although your suit jacket has several pockets, all of them should not be used.

◆ The pockets on the inside, usually in the chest area, should be used. Use them for easy access to business cards, pens, and other small items. This is also a great pocket for your Perfect Gentleman's Pocket Guide.

◆ You may also see a small, lower inside pocket, which was originally designed for holding cigarettes. I recommend not using this pocket. Putting items in this pocket will weigh your suit down on one side, which will give an awkward image or uncomfortable feel when your jacket is on. You might be able to get away with using it for a small note card or something, but minimize its use.

◆ The lower front pockets on the outside are really just for style and should not be used often. You want to minimize the use of these pockets because bulky items will affect the way your jacket looks because of weight. Yes, you can use them for light items like business cards, tickets, or a hotel room key, but really these pockets are just for style. These pockets also may have designs, be slanted or have flaps, and you do not want to take away from that look by adding bulk to these pockets.

◆ The top chest pocket, as mentioned earlier, should be used to hold your pocket square for decoration and style to complete your outfit. When convenient, also use this pocket to hold your light sunglasses or eyeglasses.

Lapels

◆ The notch lapel is the most popular. It is very simple and timeless. Choose a notch lapel for everyday wear and avoid it for formal wear.

◆ The peak lapel is when the lapel *peaks* on the chest. It gives a very rich, elegant look. It can be used with everyday wear, but it is more appropriate when choosing formal wear.

◆ The fish mouth lapel is similar to the peak lapel but a little more stylish with a space between where the peak and collar join on the lapel. It is a very nice alternative to the norm for everyday wear.

◆ The shawl lapel has no break in the fabric and wraps around your chest and collar continuously. It is very nice for tuxedos and you can wear it for everyday use if you like this style.

Vents

Vents in the suit jacket are the center or side slits in the back of a jacket. The purpose of vents is to allow for easier access to your pants back pockets when your jacket is on. If you can, I recommend choosing a jacket that has some type of vent. It looks more stylish and often times more comfortable. However, when choosing your tuxedo, it is perfectly okay to not have vents. It displays the prestige of this particular piece.

Color

♦ When beginning your suit collection, the three best colors to have are navy blue, charcoal gray and black. After these three, the possibilities are endless.

♦ Dark colors are best for suits because they are versatile. Keep in mind that the darker the suit the more elegant it will look. Conversely, the lighter color the suit the more casual.

Ferrera Fresh Tip: Choose some type of vent in your suit jacket. It will allow for a more stylish walk with your hand in your pocket.

Fabrics

In terms of fabric for your suit jacket or blazer, there is a variety of options. Among the top choices are worsted wool, tweed, herringbone, flannel, cashmere, corduroy, as well as polyester or mixed blends. Contrary to the bad reputation that polyester has, there is nothing wrong with it. However, the reason wools and other blends are recommended over polyester is because they last longer. Polyester is a man-made product and natural wool fibers quite often have a higher quality look and feel.

Cleaning & Care

When cleaning suits and blazers, some men think they need to head to the cleaners every time after wearing. Wrong! The chemicals and professional washes at the cleaners can be very harmful to natural fabrics and can cause clothing to not last as long. This does not mean that you never take your jackets to the cleaners, because you should. Depending on how often you wear it will determine how often you need to take it to professional cleaners. It just does not need to go off your back and to the cleaners after light use.

◆ After wearing your suit, try hanging the jacket and pants on separate hangers in the bathroom when taking a shower. The steam from the shower will create a dry cleaning effect that will eliminate odors.

◆ After allowing the steam to hit your suit, let it hang in an open area approximately six to eight hours before putting it back in the closet or wearing it again.

◆ If there are any spots of dirt on your fabric, use a little water and soap on a cloth to remove the spots and let air dry.

◆ For more difficult spots, point them out to the cleaners when you take it in.

◆ When you bring your clothes home from the cleaners, take them out of the protective plastic. Do not leave clothing in the plastic because it is better for wool, cotton and other natural fabrics to breathe.

Ferrera Fresh Tip: Once you have a good suit, take good care of it. If you do, you can own that same suit for many years and it will still look good!

SLACKS

Slacks, trousers, pants, or bottoms are just a few of the many different names used to describe what we as gentlemen put on our legs and wear as an outer garment. The fit of slacks is highly dependent on you, the person wearing them. Regardless of body size, they should land on your waist, which is approximately between one-half to three inches below your navel.

Fit

♦ Your slacks should land perfectly on your waist and when they are well-tailored, you should be able to wear them without a belt, even though you *should* wear a belt.

♦ The hip and crotch measurement should accent the shape of your body. When you put your slacks on, the most important thing is that you are comfortable! We all know the uncomfortable feeling of our crotch being restricted.

♦ The knee fit should be about four to five inches wider than the width of your actual knee. The cuff measurement should be about the same or a bit smaller than the knee measurement for an even flow of the fabric.

♦ If you have a large shoe size, it is often possible to widen the cuffs of your slacks and vice versa for a smaller shoe size.

♦ Remember, a good tailor or cleaners can alter the waist, knee, cuff and crotch measurements of your slacks to your liking and comfort.

Style

Pleats

Two Pleats

Pleats can give a more relaxing fit in the crotch and hip area of your slacks. Pleats in the front are great for larger gentlemen or those who want more space in their slacks. One to two pleats in the front of your slacks is enough. Three or more pleats will draw more attention to your crotch and stomach area; not to mention they'll make you look like you are 60 years old. Even if you are, your style does not have to look like it.

One Pleat

No Pleats

No Pleats, or flat front pants, give a very cool and chic look. It works great for gentlemen with slimmer body types. It accentuates your physique in your thighs, hips and butt area, which the ladies will also like. For large gentlemen or gents with wide hips, try wearing flat front pants as well. They can create a slimming effect when you wear your slacks. Pleats or no pleats depends on your comfort when wearing your pants.

Breaks

A *break* is a term used to describe how your slacks land at the cuff of your pants when worn with shoes. The area where the fabric folds or *breaks* is known as the pants break. There are three main styles to choose from: a quarter break, half break or full break. When considering which break option to choose, consult with your tailor when getting your pants altered and consider these tips in regards to your pants break:

> *Ferrera Fresh Tip:* The baggy suit and slacks will come in and go out of style, but the well-tailored James Bond style suit will be in style forever. Choose at your discretion, but I recommend the latter.

- ◆ A full break is great for tall gentlemen because it accents your height! For shorter gentlemen, the full break will make you look shorter, as if your pants are too big for you, so choose one of the other options.

Full Break

- ◆ A half break is a comfortable balance for both tall and short gentlemen. It gives a nice, even look when you are standing and when you are sitting down. It is the most common break and you can almost never go wrong with this option.

Half Break

- ◆ A quarter break is the perfect option for shorter gentlemen because it will make you look taller when standing. It is also a very stylish option for slim gentlemen and those who want to show off more of their socks when seated because your pants will rise up a little higher.

Quarter Break

Colors
- Include a variety of colors in your collection of slacks. Blue, black, gray, tan, and brown are always great colors to have, but feel free to add unusual colors and patterns to create your unique style.

Fabrics
- For slacks you have the same fabric options as in your full suits and blazers. In addition, choosing cotton is perfectly fine; it gives you a comfortable and casual look.

How to Wear
- Wear your slacks, of course, as part of your full suit, but also wear them alone with a nice dress shirt or polo.

- Style comes into play when you mix and match your slacks with different blazers. Consider a brown corduroy blazer with blue slacks or even brown khaki color slacks with a green check pattern blazer, a very PGA Masters look and style.

- Larger gentlemen should choose to wear their slacks exactly at or above their navel to keep pants securely on your waist.

- Slimmer gentlemen may choose the wear their slacks just below their actual waistline, also known as low rise. This style is contrary to classic dress, but it is appropriate and very modern-day stylish.

Cleaning & Care

♦ The fabric care of your slacks is similar to that of your sport coats and blazers.

♦ Your slacks can and should be washed or taken to the cleaners more often than your jackets. Even if you have a suit, you can take the slacks to the cleaners more often than you do the jacket.

♦ If you spill something on your slacks, spot clean it immediately with simple soap and water.

♦ Cotton, unlike wool or other types of fabric, does not require professional cleaning and can be machine washed. Make sure to read the labels inside your pants for washing instruc- tions.

Ferrera Fresh Tip: If you do choose to machine wash your cotton slacks, wash them inside out to preserve their true color.

Blazer

The blazer is similar to a suit jacket, but it is considered a blazer when the jacket is in a solid color and is paired with an unmatched pair of pants. A blazer is ideal for casual business settings, so always have it ready. Follow the same fit and styling as you would with your suit jackets. However, your blazer should be about one to one and a half inches shorter in length than a normal suit jacket. Blazers were originally

meant to represent some type of club or organization, so they often come with metal buttons that display a bit more elegance. The purpose of the blazer is for you to have a fancy, lightweight jacket to mix and match with different slacks, shirts, and even your dark denim. For style and convenience a blazer can sometimes have half-lining or no lining at all.

Sport Coat

The difference between a sport coat and a blazer is that a sport coat is for casual settings and often has some type of pattern in the fabric rather than a solid fabric of a blazer. Often times sport coats also have flap front pockets or patched front pockets. Lighter shoulder pads are also a characteristic of sport coats. Similar to the blazer, this jacket should be a little bit shorter in length. This jacket is great in fabrics like tweed,  herringbone and flannel for a very rich and cool look. The sport coat is designed to be a nice jacket that you can grab quickly out of the closet to mix and match with a variety of your slacks, shirts and jeans. The same pocket usage and style tips for your suit jacket apply for a blazer or sport coat.

Ferrera Fresh Tip: Include a variety of blazers and sports coats in your wardrobe. They will pay off handsomely by allowing you to mix and match them with other items in your closet.

SHIRTS

Like many gentlemen, you will come to learn that a well fitting, comfortable shirt is priceless. When you find a brand or a custom clothier that fits your needs, stick with it and build a relationship with that brand or company. A good shirt will not only make you look good, but you will feel good too. Invest and choose wisely to your liking; you will not regret it.

Fit

◆ The shirt should fit to complement your body type. Similar to your suit jacket, the shoulders and sleeves should match your body exactly.

◆ There should be approximately two to three inches of space between the shirt and your bicep and approximately three to five inches of space around your chest and body.

◆ The shirt length should be about eight to twelve inches lower than your waist, so that the shirt is long enough to stay tucked into your pants.

◆ The collar fit is completely dependent on the person wearing the shirt. I recommend having an exact fit for a perfect image when your tie is on. If you like a little extra breathing room at your collar, try a half-inch larger collar size.

◆ Take note that you may have to sacrifice sleeve length and fit when choosing ready-made shirts.

◆ If you have a unique body shape and you have difficulty finding a collar, sleeve length and style that work for you,

you should seriously consider custom-made shirts and other custom clothes. Tailored to your individual body type, they will last longer, look better, and feel better.

Style

When choosing shirts it can be very fun or very confusing. It becomes fun when you know what you are looking for and what you like. From collar styles, color, fit, cuff styles, and buttons, the possibilities are endless. Unfortunately, there is no "always right" or "always wrong" way to choose your shirt. It is completely up to you. If you like it, you like it, period. There are, however, a few tips to remember. As the perfect gentleman you should know:

♦   The gentleman who is fortunate enough to have a relatively even oval-shaped face can wear almost any type shirt collar, spread and point.

♦   The gentleman with a more round or circular face should opt for a shirt collar with a long point, in a classic or medium spread. This will give balance to the round face when fully dressed.

♦   The gentleman with somewhat of a rounded square face should opt for a shirt collar with a normal point or a round edge collar works well too. The medium or narrow spread collar works for this facial type as well, again for balance.

Color

When choosing colors in your shirts, start with the basics and add an infinite amount of colors. Use colors that are classic or that highlight your skin tone. However, remember that for formal events your shirt should always be white.

* Business dress shirts are great in white and hues of blue. As you enhance your style, try different patterns such as stripes and checks in blue.

* Light colors are also best for business shirts. Colors like yellow, lavender, and pink are more welcoming to the eye. Know your profession and choose wisely.

* Evening dress shirts should be just the opposite, in dark colors such as black, brown, gray, purple and similar tones, which will match perfectly in dim lights.

* Choose shirt colors that are in contrast to your tie and match your suits. However, as you become comfortable with your style, shirt and tie pairing is fun and you can do *almost* anything you want.

* When in doubt, choose colors that match with the current season or nearest holiday.

Fabrics

When choosing fabrics for your shirts, choose what is comfortable to you. The most common options are pure cotton or a cotton blend of polyester.

* Cotton is the better choice for a few reasons. First, it is a natural fiber that will give a natural look and feel. Second, cotton is soft and comfortable with a very rich look when dressed up.

- Polyester blend is a mixture of different fibers and is a nice choice for different reasons. Polyester will allow your shirts to need little or no ironing and have fewer wrinkles. It looks good and can often cost less than natural cotton shirts.

How to Wear

- A dress shirt can be worn dressed up or casual, buttoned or unbuttoned and, of course, you can wear it with a suit and tie in professional settings.

- Light colored shirts (white, blue, yellow, and lavender) are great with dark suits.

- Make sure that your shirt does not come out of your pants regularly throughout the day. It is important that your slacks fit well and that they hold your shirt in place.

- If you are wearing a shirt with removable collar stays, make sure to use the collar stays. They give a better image by keeping your collar down and maintaining a polished look.

- Opt to wear a white short-sleeve shirt under your dress shirt to avoid getting sweat from your armpits on your dress shirt.

- Wearing a white shirt underneath will also make your dress shirts look even in color and minimize unruly deodorant stains directly on your dress shirts.

- Unlike your suits, I recommend wearing a shirt only once and then it goes directly into the hamper. Shirts have direct contact with your body odors and cologne, so they should be washed after each wear.

- It is also best to have a nice amount of dress shirts. Having seven dress shirts as part of your collection will allow you to at least have one shirt for every day of the week and will minimize how often you have to do laundry.

Ferrera Fresh Tip: If you ever forget or cannot find the collar stays for your shirt, try using paper clips. They will work as well and will keep your collar down, allowing you to get through the day.

Cleaning & Care

- Use the recommended cleaning method listed on the label of the shirts you buy. Every fabric should have a description of how to care for the item.

- Shirts can be regularly machine washed or professionally cleaned. Keep in mind that the chemicals at the cleaners can be harmful to your clothes. Not to worry; there is always the enjoyment of getting new dress shirts.

- To help your shirts last longer use the normal or delicate cycle on your washing machine rather than heavy.

- If you are washing more than three dress shirts, consider washing them in their own load rather than with all the rest of your clothes.

- Prior to washing your shirts apply detergent or spot fabric cleaner on the collar to get rid of the normal heavy dirt that may be on your collar.

- If you take your shirts to the cleaners, remember to point out spots to them so that they can pay special attention to cleaning them.

> *Ferrera Fresh Tip:* Consider washing your shirts at home and only take them to the cleaners to be pressed for a crisp look. Machine wash and professional ironing will preserve the fabric quality.

VESTS

Vests are very simple pieces of the wardrobe that can easily add style or can easily be confusing. Vests can be used as the stand-out part of your outfit, or as subtle pieces to enhance your slacks, suits, and casual wear. If you find a suit that has a matching vest included, you should really consider buying it since more often than not suits are sold in only jacket and slacks. The vest will not only look good as a three-piece suit, but also it will complement other items you have as well. After you have the basics in your closet, vests can add color and style to the items you already wear. Try a variety of them and see if you like them as part of your style.

Style

There are two main types of vests for gentlemen.

* The first type is one that buttons in the front and is described as *double-breasted* vest, *notch lapel* vest or *single breasted* vest.

* The second type is known as a sweater vest, which pulls over your head like a sweater.

Ferrera Fresh Tip: When you are advanced in your style, start considering bold colors like pink or salmon vests or sweaters. Note that not all men can pull it off, but it screams confidence with the ladies when you can!

Colors

* Gray, black with pinstripe, and tan are great starters for wool, suit-style vests. These colors give a nice variety to pair them with your slacks, and even denim to dress up your outfit a bit.

* Black, gray, and red are great starter colors when considering sweaters and vests because they are very versatile.

* Orange, light green, pastel yellow and powder blue all work as colors in cashmere or cotton vests and sweaters.

* In addition to these colors, try using some patterns and designs; stripes and checks work great.

Fabrics

* Since you may wear vests with your suits, slacks and denim, know that you can utilize a variety of different wools, cottons, and cashmeres.

* Contrary to popular opinion, the vest fabric does not have to match the suit exactly. It looks great when it matches, but it certainly does *not have* to.

How to Wear

* Wear your vest, as mentioned, with suits, slacks, jeans, or even in the spring with khaki shorts.

* Pair a vest with a nice dress shirt underneath. If the shirt has a pattern in it already, try to use an opposite patterned vest, or better yet, wear a solid color vest. Do the opposite if your shirt is a solid color.

* V-neck vests are great because you can show off your shirt underneath and it also allows you to wear neckties or bowties.

* In the fall and winter, wear the vest with your full suit to keep your body warmer.

* In the spring and summer, ditch the suit jacket and wear the vest alone with your slacks and dress shirt. This will not only present a professional image, but also it will keep your body cooler.

Cleaning & Care

* If the vest is wool, polyester, corduroy or other suit fabric, follow the dab-and-clean process as in suits.

* Cashmere and other cottons should be hand washed and air-dried or professionally cleaned.

SHOES

A nice pair of dress shoes should never be overlooked in your wardrobe. Unfortunately, some men often focus on their nice suit or clothes, and pay no attention to completing the outfit with nice shoes. The perfect gentleman, however, should never overlook this part of the outfit. Your shoes do not have to be drastically expensive, but I would recommend paying attention to detail and invest in a pair of shoes you really like so that you do not have to continue replacing them. Shoes are the one piece that play a very important part in your style and comfort throughout the day, so choose a good pair.

Fit

* Unless your body is still drastically growing, get shoes that fit your feet exactly. Shoes that are too big or too small can hurt and leave uncomfortable blisters on your feet.

* There should be no visible space between your sock and the side, back or tongue of the shoe, unless you are wearing a boot dress shoe.

- Your shoes should match the shape of your foot. If you have a wide foot, choose a shoe designed for wide feet and vice versa for narrow feet.

- If you have a hard time feeling comfortable in dress shoes, a cobbler or shoe repair professional may be able to alter your shoe or add extra cushion inside for comfort. Another option is custom footwear, which will match your foot perfectly.

> *Ferrera Fresh Tip:* You may want to start building a relationship with the shoe salesperson so you can always go to him or her for shoes when you need a new pair.

Style

- Different leathers, suede, fabrics and textures are a great way to add style.

- Cow leather is the most popular, but alligator, crocodile (there is a difference), shark, and others are very stylish as well.

- Lace-up shoes are nice because you can wear them in both formal and casual settings. Lace-up dress shoes should be one of the first pair of shoes you own.

- Slip-on shoes are great casual dress type shoes. The darker and shinier the shoe the dressier it will look. Wear them accordingly.

- *What if I don't have any dress shoes?* Wear the darkest shoes you have. Make sure they are clean, and get a pair of dress shoes as soon as possible. You can also rent dress shoes from a tuxedo shop as needed.

Color

* Black leather is a must. It will always be classy and you can wear black shoes with almost anything.

* Dark brown is the next color to add. From there, add burgundy, different shades of black and brown, gray, green, and any other colors you like.

PANTS TO SHOE COLOR GUIDE

Suit or Pants Color is…	Shoe Color Should be…
Black	Black, Camel Brown
Navy	Black, Brown or Burgundy
Gray	Black, Dark Brown or Burgundy
Brown	Brown Shades or Black
White	White, Black, or Dark Brown

Fabrics

* Opt for leather dress shoes as much as possible. Man-made leather products have come a long way and, in fact, can look good. But genuine leather often looks better and lasts longer.

* I emphasize this point on genuine leather because it is great if your shoes last a very long time. Yes, it may cost more in the beginning. However, it will ultimately

cost less, since you will not be replacing shoes every three months due to wear and tear or because they are uncomfortable.

- Leather soled shoes are often able to be replaced by a local shoe repair or personal cobbler.

- Suede is great for shoes too. In my opinion, suede simply looks fresh and can last long as well.

- For colder weather, rubber soled shoes can be very beneficial. Rubber does not absorb water so when there is rain or snow, rubber soled shoes are your best bet.

How to Wear

- Your shoes should always be clean.

- Shine and polish your shoes regularly in order to prolong the quality and life of your shoes.

- If the shoe is a lace up, wear it that way and if it is a buckle shoe, fasten it to your liking.

- Mix and match them with your whole wardrobe. Pair dark slacks with dark shoes, brown slacks with brown shoes, etc.

- When you are comfortable with your style, you can take risks. There is nothing wrong with wearing brown shoes with blue slacks or black shoes with brown slacks.

- Be confident in your shoe selection and pairing. Regardless of your shoes, your character will still allow you to display yourself as the perfect gentleman.

Clean & Care

- Rather than using water and soap to clean dress shoes, use a cleaner designed specifically for that type of shoe, such as leather or suede.

- Consider resoling your shoes when they begin to feel uncomfortable or somehow different than when you normally wear them.

- Just as you do with your cleaners, build a relationship with a cobbler, the person who shines, resoles, and takes care of your shoes. This relationship is valuable and will save you money from having to repurchase new shoes.

Ferrera Fresh Tip: Carry a pocket shoe shiner in your glove box or briefcase and give your shoes a wipe down before entering a business meeting or event.

ACCESSORIES

Accessories are often used more by women, but the right accessories are appropriate for the perfect gentleman as well. Cuff links, belts, suspenders, lapel pins, and watches are not only nice "finishing touches," but also they are items you will need to complete your outfits. For example, you *must have* cuff links to wear a French cuff shirt or you will *need* a belt or suspenders to hold your pants on your waist. Add additional accessories to your wardrobe and choose to start a collection of them if you would like. Just be mindful that collecting accessories such as cuff links or watches can become addicting and costly. However, it will pay off handsomely to your style.

Belts

As mentioned earlier, opt for good leather in your belts because they will last long. After you have the black and dark brown leather belt, *then* you can add suede and other fabrics. Matching your belt with your shoes is timeless in your business attire. However, matching belts with other parts of your clothing is a bit more exciting and edgy for leisure attire. For example, matching your green fabric belt with your green boat shoes is completely appropriate. As your wardrobe grows, be stylish in matching your watchband leather with your belt and shoes, match gold or silver buckles on your belt with your shoe buckles and watch metals. Consider even matching your ink pen and briefcase metals to your attire after your wardrobe has really expanded.

Suspenders

Suspenders are not used often these days, which makes it a very out-of-the-ordinary, stylish accessory. When wearing suspenders there is no need to wear a belt. Suspenders and belts serve the same purpose of holding your pants on your waist. Adjust the straps so they fit comfortably around your shoulders and do not pull your pants too far on your crotch. Suspenders are great when it is hard to find a belt your size. Remember to use similar styles as your belts. Different fabric and style suspenders are great as well.

Ties

I am not sure which I like more, watches or ties. The important thing to know is that ties can turn an ordinary suit into an extraordinary outfit! As you continually enhance your tie collection, here are 10 Ferrera Fresh Tips that will guarantee confidence in your necktie wearing:

1. Wear what you like! Do not chase trends or try to match and mirror what everyone else around you is doing. Sticking to your style will create your individual image.

2. Opt for silk neckties more often than not. In my opinion, silk ties are a great option because they look good, feel good and last long. Woven silk, printed silk or plain silk all work. Knit fabric ties are an occasional nice alternative, but silk always works. Silk ties are available almost everywhere and have a wide price range for your convenience.

3. A good knot will make for a good look. A tie is just a piece of fabric until it is tied correctly, neat and even. Take time to make sure your tie's knot is in the middle of your collar. Make sure your tie does not twist and turn to the backside of the tie continuously. If it does, this means you should retie it so that it is straight. A good knot is one that is firm and stays in place.

4. Tie the right knot for your shirt style. In addition to tying a good knot, tie the *right* knot appropriate for your shirt. It can look awkward when the wrong knot is used for a particular shirt collar. A narrow spread or button-down collar is best with a four-in-hand knot. A medium spread collar is nice with a four-in-hand knot,

half-Windsor knot, or a Pratt knot. A wide spread collar can welcome any knot and is perfect for a full Windsor knot, which will give you a wide and stylish finish at your collar. *(See page 77.)*

5. Do not leave your ties tied after you wear them. I know that you have never done this, but some guys, not the perfect gentleman, tie their ties once and then loosen it enough to take the tie off over their head so the knot is remains. That way they do not have to tie the tie again the next time they wear it. This is horrible for your tie because it will damage the quality. Do not do this. When you are finished with your tie, undo it and then roll it up or hang it neatly.

6. Have a variety of colors and styles! Patterns and stripes will always work. Wearing novelty ties with characters or figures is a bit more tricky because you do not want to look like a kid in a man's world. However, if you like them, wear them and ask for thoughts from others whose opinion you respect. Bright colors, paisleys, polka dots, stripes and everything else are all good options. You can even mix and match patterns if you choose to. (A whole other chapter can be written about that, but I'll stop for now.) Choose the ties in your collection wisely. You can never have too many ties, and if you do, start giving them away to other gentlemen or students who can put them to use.

7. Minimize wearing the exact same shirt and suit with the exact same tie. I know this can be difficult for some gents, but alternating, mixing and matching your ties and

shirt will make you look like you have a lot more clothes and more importantly, it will show that you know *how* to dress. You do not want to look like a super hero that wears the same thing all the time. You want to look like you have style. Ask for help from other stylish people or your lady, if you need to.

8. Wear your tie at the right length. The end of your tie should land right in the middle of your belt buckle. This will give you a perfectly even image when you are standing or seated. If your tie is too long or too short, retie it. Do not tuck your tie into your pants because it is too long. Also do not have the silky part show longer than the wide part when finished. If you choose to wear your tie in any different way, you are on your own; it's not recommended.

9. Avoid wearing exact patterns in your tie and pocket square. This is just too elementary. Well, you can do it, but it is not the most stylish thing to do. It is too boring and can make you look like you have a very old school style of dress. By wearing similar colors in your pocket square and tie will give a bit more style and character to your whole outfit.

10. Keep your ties clean. Dirty ties are just disgusting and so inappropriate for the perfect gentleman. If you ever spill something on your tie, do not panic. Your tie might not be ruined. Try to get the spot off immediately. Use light water, if needed, and let it air dry. Then take it to the cleaners when you can and they should be able to take care of it. If you put on a tie that you notice is dirty, clean it or do not wear it.

HOW TO TIE A TIE

Four-in-Hand Knot:

1. Start by placing the tie around your collar with the small part about two inches above your waistline.

2. Cross the wide side over the small side and wrap it around, returning to the original side.

3. Now wrap the wide part over the front of the knot being formed.

4. Take the wide end underneath and through the space closest to your neck.

5. Pull it down through the front to tie the knot.

6. Snug tightly to your collar, straighten and you're set!

For more knot styles, see *Chapter 10,*
The Perfect Gentleman Knows How To...

Bowties

Bowties are a nice alternative to the normal necktie. If you choose to wear them regularly as your signature style, by all means, you can. It is not uncommon for a man to not know how to tie a bowtie, so don't panic. However, as the perfect gentleman you *should* know how. The PGPG will be your guide or refresher, but it is better to have someone teach you. Ask a sales associate who you buy your bowtie from to teach you or someone that you know personally. Take note that clip-on or ready-made bowties are okay, but it is a bit more refined when you have a bowtie you actually know how to tie.

HOW TO TIE A BOWTIE

Start by adjusting the length of the bowtie to match your neck collar size. Note: A longer bowtie will make a larger bow and vice versa.

1. Place the tie around collar with one end about one inch and a half longer than the other.

2. Now cross the longer end over the smaller and through the area closest to your neck.

3. Pull to fit snug the ends back to the same sides. (There will be no adjusting this part after you're done, so snug it close.)

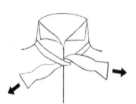

4. Now form the front part of the bow by folding the small end and placing it over the center and hold it in place.

5. Now take the longer end and wrap it over the front bow you just formed and take the wide area of the longer end to wrap it.

6. Now pass it through the side loop area behind the front bow. (You cannot always see this area but can feel it)

7. Adjust, straighten and form your bowtie and you're set. A little practice and you'll be a bowtie-tying champ.

Ascot

The ascot, or cravat, is a piece of neckwear that is to be worn as a more informal, "just style" piece. It is a very short and wide fabric, often in silk. The ascot is tied around your neck on the inside of your shirt and shown through the unbuttoned collar of your shirt. It is a

Ferrera Fresh Tip: Wearing an ascot or even owning one is completely up to you. Just like cuff links, an ascot does not say anything about your status. If you like it, wear it and enjoy!

very stylish way to avoid wearing a tie in casual social settings. Ascots have a long history dating back to the 1700s with British royalty and some gents still consider it a fashionable statement. Avoid wearing an ascot for important business engagements.

HOW TO TIE AN ASCOT

1. Start with one side longer than the other.

2. Cross the longer end over the shorter and wrap it under, bringing it back to the original side.

3. Wrap the longer part over the center.

4. Now take the longer part underneath through the open space closest to your neck.

5. Finish by bringing the same piece to the front and remaining on the top. Then tuck it inside your shirt and fluff it to your liking.

Watches

Watches are a wonderful accessory for the perfect gentleman and can be inexpensive or very pricey, depending on quality, style and brand. You will get to the elaborate expensive watch, but start with a classic watch that can be worn on many different occasions to accomplish the job of telling the time.

* I recommend opting for a silver stainless steel watch as you start your collection. Stainless steel is light and durable, while silver will make your watch versatile, allowing you to wear it in causal or dressy settings.

* A leather band watch is nice as well because you can change the band as it wears, basically giving you a watch you can own for life.

* Wear your watch on your left hand. Some thieves steal watches right off the wrists of people when shaking their hands. Since we often shake with the right hand, wearing your watch on the left wrist minimizes the chance for wristwatch theft. In addition, it will make your wrist less bulky when shaking hands.

> *Ferrera Fresh Tip*: Plan to invest in a nice watch. Know that whatever you invest in a watch you like, it is well worth the money.

Bracelets

Bracelets can be in fancy metals or in simple materials, promoting an organization or a reminder of life. They are usually worn on the right wrist since the watch is on the left hand, but it is all personal preference. Just be mindful when wearing fancy jewelry. The perfect gentleman does not need to boldly show off. People worth taking notice will notice. Keep it clean and enjoy it.

Necklace

Necklaces or chains are a complete personal preference and they are a very flashy item for a gentleman. If you are wearing a chain with a collar shirt, you can wear it under the fold of the collar, allowing the chain to show. Avoid the large diamonds or gold chains for business settings unless it is part of your profession. Such chains will be too distracting to people you interact with. Wearing a chain at leisure or social events is more appropriate for the perfect gentleman.

Rings

Rings usually have significance and can denote a position or stature. Some rings identify you as a member of an organization. Wear rings if you choose to. If you are married, wear your wedding band proudly. While conducting business, try not to wear too many rings on your right hand, since it can be uncomfortable to you and others when shaking hands. Also, in corporate environments, lose the pinky ring. Many times people associate a pinky ring with the sly criminals in movies and that is not an image you want to portray as the perfect gentleman in business.

Earrings

About 50 years ago this would have not even been a topic concerning the male wardrobe. However, times have changed and I must address it. The most important thing to remember if you wear earrings is to keep them clean. I recommend taking your earrings out for job interviews and initial business interactions. This will eliminate prejudgments toward you.

The same goes for your eyebrows, nose, tongue, and whatever else you have pierced around your face. Once you are seasoned in your profession and your value is known far more than your perception, earrings may be more acceptable, so please be mindful as the perfect gentleman.

> *Ferrera Fresh Tip:* Always consider your profession and wear earrings accordingly. Earrings are not bad, and frankly can be cool, but it is completely up to you what image you want to portray.

Lapel Pin

Lapel pins are intended to be worn on the lapel of your suit jacket or blazer, not on your topcoat. Plus, most of the time a lapel pin is not sturdy enough to go through the heavy material of a topcoat. Since most lapel pins symbolize something of importance, it should be worn on your left lapel at the buttonhole to give the image that the pin is near your heart and represents something you care about. The same applies if you are wearing multiple pins or ribbons. They all should go on your left lapel. If you are a part of some private society or organization that has a special pin, understand the rules of how you are to wear the pin and wear it accordingly. Lapel pin etiquette does not apply in this situation.

Name Badges

Name badges, whether hand written or printed, should be worn on the right lapel or right chest area of the outer most part of your attire. If you are wearing a coat indoors, wear your name badge there. Most people read from left to right and when they look at you, your name badge is naturally seen because our minds are accustomed to seeing and reading from left to right.

Boutonnière

Boutonnières or floral decoration on your lapel is another way to add style. It is not common for men to wear them on the everyday business suit, but I highly recommend it for fancy events such as an evening ball or special occasion. Sometimes, wear one just because no one else is doing it. It may cause others to step their game up at the next event and cause you to subtly stand out among the other gents who also are well-dressed. Wear it on the left lapel at the button-hole of your suit jacket or blazer.

1. When pinning it on your lapel, start by holding the flower in place where you want it to stay.

2. Then, start the pin from the back side of the lapel to the front and through the large part of the flower stem.

3. Now bring the tip of the pin back into and underneath the lapel, so that it is hidden and will not poke anyone you hug throughout the night.

4. You're set and ready to go!

Cuff Links

Cuff links are just cool in my opinion. Some gentlemen will enjoy them and others will not because they can be too much of a hassle, they are easily misplaced, or costly. Like Dr. Seuss says in the book *Green Eggs & Ham*, "Try them! Try them!" If you like them, opt for French cuff shirts to wear them. Choose from the cufflink options you like since they can be very stylish and come in many different shapes, sizes, colors, and designs. You can even get a custom pair. Cuff links can be collectible jewelry, which you can easily grow fond of, like I have.

It is completely okay if you do not like them. Cuff links say nothing about status. I know plenty of wealthy individuals who simply hate wearing them. Whether you wear them or not is a personal preference. Remember that your cuff links look great when they match the color of your belt buckle, watch, or other colors you are wearing. Although you can wear cuff links with your everyday attire, *Ferrera Fresh Tip*: For some reason, ladies like a gentleman in a nice pair of cuff links! Take note and you might get a little more attention with this small enhancement. you definitely should wear cuff links with your tuxedo. Cuff links bring a bit more elegance to the attire when you have them on with a tuxedo.

Shirt Studs

Shirt studs are usually worn for very elegant occasions such as your wedding day or during a black tie or tuxedo event. You can get away with not wearing them if you are wearing a necktie covering the front of your shirt. However, if you are wearing a bowtie and your shirt has stud holes, wear the studs. Put the studs in each hole. The smaller shiny end is the part that should show on the front of your shirt. You do not need to put studs in the buttonholes of the shirt that is tucked into your pants. No one will see them anyway (at least in public). Remember to take care of them, as they can easily get lost. Once you finish wearing them, I would recommend putting them in a small box or the case they came in.

Cummerbund

The cummerbund is a wide waist band similar to a belt, which is primarily for dressing up your tuxedo. It is intended to replace a waistcoat, also known as a vest for tuxedos. I recommend going with the vest because the cummerbund is an old military style way of dress. If you do wear one, remember two things. First, a quarter width of the cummerbund should cover the waistband of your pants. Second, the pleats should be turned up, so that you can hold small things in the pleats like a pocket for money or a ring.

Tie Clip

Tie clips, tie bars, tie chains, and tie pins are all necktie accessories to hold your necktie in place. From my research, the tie clip looks best when it has no design and is one solid color like gold, silver or black. Tie clips are to be clipped on the front of the tie together with the underlining shirt. For the young individuals, I would avoid using clips with chains or anything that dangles. It looks very out dated and it will take attention away from the coolness of your tie.

Once your wardrobe has matured, a tie clip or tie pin can be a nice chic accessory. If you are like me and hate your tie moving all over the place, try using a device like *The Tie Lock*. This little device clips to the backside of your tie, then clips to your shirt, making it invisible while it holds your tie securely in place. Whichever option you choose, make sure your tie is in place to your liking.

Hats

Hats are long gone as part of everyday attire for men, but they are appropriate to wear depending on your location and weather you experience. The primary purpose of a hat is to protect you from the weather. For example, a hat can provide shade on a sunny day or  protect you from the rain. The secondary purpose is for style. Although, I guess that could be said about all other pieces or clothing. A fedora, a top hat, trucker hat or a baseball hat all can be nice accessories, and contrary to popular opinion, you *can* wear hats inside.

♦ In casual settings like football games or hangouts with friends and family, it is okay to leave your hat on indoors. If your hat is a part of your outfit as the perfect gentleman or representing something in relation to your social event, it is also okay to be worn indoors.

♦ When wearing a hat it is courteous for a gentleman to tip his hat with a nod of the head when meeting a lady as well as a gentleman. You do not need to remove the hat completely, as in the past. But a modern day touch and nod is appropriate.

- You can eat with your hat on in a bar or while eating finger food on a couch. However, always remove your hat when eating at any organized table setting.

- Finally, you never have to remove any religious headwear unless you choose, and you should never ask someone to do so either.

Umbrella

Depending on where you live in the world, a good umbrella could be a necessity. Not only will the umbrella protect you and the lady you are with from unpleasant weather, but it can complement your style as a cool accessory as well. When choosing, it is almost hard for me to suggest any other color than black. Black is classic and will match with almost anything, including that pea coat you just added. The one thing to make sure of is that it is large enough to protect you. A golf style umbrella is great because, as a gentleman, it can give you the opportunity to share it with someone else when necessary.

Eyewear

If eyeglasses are prescribed to you, you should wear them. In fact, they can be a very stylish accessory. Eyeglasses are a great accessory to draw focus to your face when  communicating with people. I spoke with a friend, William Gordon, a custom eyewear designer for almost ten years at *Eye Was Framed*, and he shared a few tips for the perfect gentleman to use when selecting eyewear. Mr. Gordon suggests that rather than getting glasses that match your face, get a pair that complements your face.

+ The shape of your glasses should be opposite of the shape of your face. For example, the gentleman who is fortunate to have an oval-shaped face has the benefit of wearing almost any shaped frame. The gentleman who has a round or circular shaped face should opt for a rectangular shaped frame in order to give a balanced image to the facial area. Likewise, the gentleman with a somewhat wider, square-shaped face should opt for round-shaped frames, again to give balance to your face.

+ Ask for guidance and recommendations in the store or someone who will give you an honest opinion. "It is too important for you to have glasses that you truly enjoy," says Mr. Gordon.

Ferrera Fresh Tip: Add multiple specs to your accessory collection and alternate between them to match with your attire and style for any particular occasion.

Sunglasses

Sunglasses, shades, frames, or whatever you personally call them, are a great accent to all outfits in the sun. I recommend owning two different pairs of sunglasses: a brown pair to match with your brown shoes, belts and so on, and a black pair that you can wear with anything. Protect them by keeping them in a case. I am not a fan of wearing sunglasses at night or indoors. The reason some celebrities wear sunglasses indoors is entertainers are sometimes under intense lights or camera flashes and sunglasses at night can help to minimize the glare. You decide what you want to do, but please know that the perfect gentleman is cool enough without them.

PREPARED WITH STYLE

In addition to having stylish attire, the perfect gentleman is always prepared for situations that could come up in life. Therefore, the perfect gentleman must be prepared with the perfect pockets. In this section you will find a few things you as the perfect gentleman should keep handy. Here are the items that will allow you to be prepared.

Mobile Device

♦ With the new era of technology we live in, one of the most important things to have handy is a mobile device or cell phone. I mean, it connects us to almost everything. It can be used to take notes, get directions, help someone in emergencies, exchange electronic business cards and much more.

♦ Keep your mobile device handy in a pocket that is easily accessible and remember that the perfect gentleman does not need to show off his flashy mobile device for any reason.

Ferrera Fresh Tip: Make sure your mobile device works for you. There is no need for a $500 phone when you use only $40 worth of its capabilities.

Wallet

♦ Your wallet is, of course, to hold identification cards, money, credit cards and other necessities. Regardless of how often we use technological currency like credit cards or debit cards, the perfect gentleman should have some cash ready and available. You never know when you will need to offer a cash tip or assist someone in need.

> *Ferrera Fresh Tip*: Consider using a money clip or a no-fold wallet that just holds your necessities. A business card holder is also a neat and simple way to hold cards and money.

Pen

◆ The ink pen is perfect for business and leisure for taking quick notes or exchanging information.

◆ It does not need to be an expensive pen. However, it does need to look nice and write smoothly to your liking.

◆ A nice pen complements your style.

◆ People appreciate when you can lend them a pen.

◆ Make sure your pen does not have chewed caps, bite marks or anything else that looks sloppy.

◆ Black or blue ink is best for simple, everyday use. Avoid any other color. It is simply more mature to use black or blue ink.

> *Ferrera Fresh Tip*: Carry two pens. You never know when a pen will run out of ink. Also, with two pens you'll be able to lend one to another person in need, while still using yours.

Mints

◆ Mints are great for a quick mouth refresher just before a meeting or when approaching a wonderful lady.

◆ I recommend choosing mints rather than gum, because chewing can be a distraction while you are talking in business or social settings.

- Also, remember that in some places chewing gum may not even be allowed in the building.

- Mints also can be refreshing to keep you alert during a boring meeting.

- When sharing mints with others, let them pick their mint. Do not place the mint into their hand, unless it is individually wrapped.

Ferrera Fresh Tip: Small powerful mints are great. They take up minimal space in your pocket and get the job done.

Handkerchief

- A tissue or handkerchief is so appropriate to have in the case of a sneeze, cough, or a spill that may happen.

- Carry it in your inside jacket pocket or pants pocket for easy access. Once you have used your handkerchief or tissue, discreetly fold it neatly and place it back into your pocket.

- If you are using tissue, throw it away when you can and grab a new one to replace the one you have used.

Ferrera Fresh Tip: Wash your hands as soon as you can after using your tissue or handkerchief. Of the two options, I would recommend using tissue and replacing it after use.

Lip Balm

◆ Oh, yes! Lip balm, ChapStick or whatever you want to call it should always be readily available to the perfect gentleman.

◆ As a gentleman you are speaking with people on a regular basis and your lips may get dry and uncomfortable. Grab the ChapStick, apply a few swipes, and you're back in the game.

◆ You also may want to keep a back-up in places where you are often such as in your vehicle or at your office.

> *Ferrera Fresh Tip*: Ditch ChapStick with flavors, colors, or gloss. Leave that to the ladies, gents!

The PGPG

◆ The arguable seventh item to have is The Perfect Gentleman's Pocket Guide.

◆ The PGPG is designed to fit in your pocket for quick access. It will help you navigate through many experiences of life.

◆ Have it handy to reference and to share with others. You never know when you can bless someone else or when you many need a quick reminder.

> *Ferrera Fresh Tip*: Own it. Have it. Use it. The Perfect Gentleman's Pocket Guide, that is.

The other things you carry like keys, sunglasses, pocket watch, notepad, or tickets to a game or show can all be carried in a briefcase or in one hand until you get to your destination. You can slip them in a pocket for a short time, but you really want to limit the things in your pockets as much as possible. This will not only keep the shape of your clothes intact, but also will not weigh you down. Having a heavy arsenal of items on you will make you inaccessible and not as free to move around when needed. Keys are important, so keep them to the few keys you actually use.

In the fashion and style wrap-up, remember to embrace your style, gents. Some of us are born with it and for some of us style must be learned. This chapter is your guide to essentials and ideas to enhance your style. As the perfect gentleman it is important to remember that you do not dress for the approval of others; dress for your own enjoyment and to your own liking. The age-old statement that says when you look good you feel good is as true as the sky is blue and I recommend using style to your advantage. Ladies will appreciate a well-dressed gentleman as will your employer, clients and others. Regardless of how well you dress, as the perfect gentleman it is important to know that people should not remember you for your clothes, but for the graceful person that you are inside the clothes.

EVENT DRESS ETIQUETTE GUIDE

The Event Says	The Perfect Gentleman Wears
Black Tie	Tuxedo or black suit only
White Tie	Suit or tuxedo with white tie
Black Tie Optional	Dark suit or tuxedo
Business Attire	Suit and tie
Business Casual	Dress slacks and shirt (jacket optional)
Semiformal	Dark suit and tie
Cocktail Attire	Slacks, dress shirt and jacket optional
Dressy Casual	Blazer, dress shirt, corduroy or dark denim
Casual	Jeans, shirt, shorts or attire of choice
Theme Attire	Dress as specified

4
The Perfect Gentleman
Communicates Well

The perfect gentleman knows that communication is the most important aspect of any relationship. With family, friends, ladies, or in business, communication in a relationship is the cement connecting the bricks of a strong wall. In this section of The PGPG you will find helpful hints for appropriate and effective communicating, whether face to face, by phone, electronically and through social media outlets like Facebook, Twitter or Linkedin. Statistics have shown that 93% of communication is not the actual words you say. Tone, body language, and *how* the statements are presented have more impact on the recipient. When communicating, be mindful of the tips here in The PGPG and use them to your advantage when communicating.

Ferrera Fresh Tip: You are always communicating, even when you are not speaking. Be mindful of that, gentlemen.

Face-to-Face

Face-to-face communication engages almost all the senses of hearing, sight, smell, and sometimes includes touch. When communicating face to face the perfect gentleman knows:

* Eye contact is essential when communicating with both ladies and other gentlemen. It shows sincerity in your communication. It also shows you are confident in your communication skills.

* Great posture when standing or sitting allows your words to be more clear and crisp when talking to others.

* Minimize shifting weight, slouching in chairs, and random unnecessary movements; it simply distracts the listener.

* Presentable attire is always appropriate in face-to-face communication. As stated in the style section, always look your best in public.

* Unless it is your signature look, eliminate mustache and beard hair from *covering* your mouth. This does not mean you cannot wear them, because you can; just keep it neat. Keep in mind a well-shaved, good-looking man can be a distraction when communicating with ladies. But that might be a good thing for you; just stay focused.

* Only use your hands while talking when it will help communicate what you are saying. Useless hand movements are distracting to the listener.

- When listening, actually *listen* so you can respond intelligently. Motions to agree or disagree, stillness, facial expressions, and eye contact apply as well. Use gestures only when appropriate while you are listening so that it shows the person talking that you are listening.

Ferrera Fresh Tip: If you are talking to someone who is blind or has difficulty hearing, look and talk in their direction. It helps them focus on your voice. Many times their listening skills are very sharp.

On the Phone

Phone communication can be very effective in the up-tempo lifestyle of the perfect gentleman. When communicating on his home phone, office phone, or cell phone the perfect gentleman knows to:

- Be a good listener. Since you do not have the advantages of face-to-face interaction, it is important to focus on the conversation to respond appropriately.

- Minimize checking emails, talking to others, and miscellaneous activities when on the phone with someone. It's just rude, if done often.

- Talk clear and crisp, especially on cell phones and earpieces, which can pick up a lot of additional background noises.

- Talk in an appropriate volume. A phone conversation is between the people on the call, not the whole world. The person near you does not need to hear your conversation, which can be a rude and unwanted distraction.

- Take calls only when you have time to talk or want to talk, and always remember to return calls you do not take at the time.

- Use speakerphone only when the conversation does not involve sensitive information. Inform the other person they are "now on speakerphone" and kindly take a person off if they ask.

- Try to end all calls on a positive note since you cannot see facial expressions or body language.

> *Ferrera Fresh Tip:* When you are solo or in private, you can talk and laugh as loud as you want on the phone, but always remember to talk in a respectable volume when on the phone in public.

Phone Messages

When leaving a phone message for someone, the perfect gentleman knows:

- All the "on the phone" etiquette applies.

- Leave your return call number twice so the person does not have to rewind the message. For example: This is (Your Name) and my phone number is… (insert your phone message). Again, this is (Your Name) and my phone number is…"

- Keep your message short. Make the recipient want to talk to the perfect gentleman. Unless you are leaving detailed information he or she has asked for, 20 to 40 seconds is enough time to get your information across.

- When leaving a message for a person to take action and you do not need a call back, you can take a little longer.

- When leaving a message always complete the message, even if you feel you have made a mistake in the middle. All message systems do not have the erase feature. But if it does, use it when you make a mistake.

- Have positive energy when leaving a message, even when the call is not necessarily the most exciting news.

- The perfect gentleman *always* returns calls. It is also appropriate to have an assistant return calls for you.

- With so many ways of communication, there is *almost* no excuse not to get back to someone. A 48-hour window is enough time, even for the busiest man in the world.

- When you return calls, return them in order of importance, then in the order received.

Ferrera Fresh Tip: A phone message can impact whether a person wants to call you back or not. Be strategic and use subtle excitement when indicating importance of information. Make the person you are calling want to call you back.

Electronic Communication

E-mail has become a very popular way of communicating with people in business and personal relationships. One of the most important things to be mindful of as the perfect gentleman with e-communication is to understand that an email can be the first interaction you have with someone. Therefore, always present yourself at best in your e-communication. When using email the perfect gentleman knows to:

- Proofread ALL emails. Whether business or pleasure emails, please proofread your email, even if it's a short reply. We all have typos now and again, but they should not happen often. Your message is more powerful with little to no errors.

- Make sure you are sending emails to the right people, including Carbon Copy (CC) and Blind Carbon Copy (BCC). If an error email is sent, send a message to that person asking them to kindly delete and confirm.

- Remember, once an email is sent, it is public information. You do not know who can or will read the message, so be respectful when sending emails.

- Be aware that email may be the first or only communication you have with someone, so preserve your image.

- When you receive emails, make sure to actually read them. Your response can tell the person if you read the email or not. Note that some emails do not require a response but rather an action or instructions.

- If asked to respond with a phone call or by any other means, respond accordingly. Do not use email to escape a conversation or an action task.

- Do not use ALL CAPITAL LETTERS IN YOUR WHOLE EMAIL. It looks like you are yelling at the person reading the email.

* Ditch shorthand and symbols in professional emails such as: BTW—By The Way, LOL–Laugh Out Loud, or smiley faces :-) You are a professional gentleman and should only use shorthand with people you have a good relationship with.

Ferrera Fresh Tip: Flirting is a big "no-no" in corporate emails. It only should be done respectfully in private settings or in private emails, since you still do not know who can read them.

* Your email is like a desk. Keep it clean, clear and organized. The cleaner it is, the more effective you can be.

* Be respectful of other people's inbox with foolish forwards and spam. Forward emails only when you think the recipient can benefit from the message.

* With mobile email, laptops, and other technology devices, appropriate time to respond to emails is within forty-eight hours, just like a phone calls, unless you need to do research.

* If you are on vacation or unable to answer email for a long period of time, use an auto message to explain your scheduled absence or unresponsiveness.

* If a message requires more of your time before you can respond, send a simple reply saying so and move on.

* Never use email when a phone call or face meeting can be more effective. Use email to set up the appointment.

- Do not use email to settle arguments. No tone, feeling, or expression can be perceived through email and statements easily can be misunderstood. As the perfect gentleman, pick up the phone and resolve the problem.

Text Message

Text message communication should be used only as a convenience, not as a means of "conversation." Short Message Service (SMS) should be just that, short information that is effective or enjoyable to the recipient. Text messaging is similar to a short email and should be treated that way, with a bit more flexibility. When using text messages a gentleman knows:

- Be creative so that your message is not too long while still getting the information across.

- Determine or ask associates and friends whether they prefer to receive text messages and respond to them accordingly.

- Text messaging is for short messages when a person is unable to talk.

- Do not use text messages as a means to have full conversations unless there is a specific reason.

- Do not use text messaging as a form of talking while in meetings. You may get by with one or two short messages, explaining that you're in a meeting, but do not abuse text messaging while in meetings.

♦ Shorthand is fine for text messages such as, "BTW, can u c if we have eggs?"

♦ Treat text messages like a short email and use the same etiquette. Text messaging can be very helpful or can be very annoying. Be respectful to people's time and use it when effective.

Ferrera Fresh Tip: Sometimes a short phone call is better than texting. Most people can speak faster than they can type and listen faster than they can read. Choose wisely.

Instant Messaging

Instant messaging, video conferencing, or live chatting should be treated as a combination of phone, email or face-to-face communication. Respond accordingly using all of the above tips.

Social Media

Social media communication would not even have been a topic in an etiquette book 20 years ago. But, since times have changed, the perfect gentlemen must adjust accordingly. Social media like Facebook, Twitter, YouTube, Linkedin and others are powerful and fun ways to stay connected with old friends, create new ones and interact for business. When making social media interaction fun and effective the perfect gentleman knows:

♦ Be respectful! Social media is a great way to meet new people and expand networks. Being respectful to others is part of that expansion.

- Other people may be able to see your social media communication so keep that in mind. You never know if someone is using social media solely for personal or for business and you never want to hamper their image in any way.

- You do not need to put everyone's personal business in the view of the public. Personal pictures and private activities should sometimes remain that way.

- A good idea when posting pictures on social media is to simply let the person know what you plan to post by communicating with them. Take note on how they respond and reply respectfully to their wishes.

- Be the perfect gentleman on social media. You know what should and should not be exposed to the public.

- Use social media as a means to learn more about people, including their activities and interests. That knowledge will allow you to interact better during face-to-face conversations with people.

- Social media can also make a business relationship stronger by knowing the person more. You can treat someone to birthday gifts, dinner reservations or other surprises, once you know what they enjoy.

- Remember, you do not have to comment or reply to everything on social media. Likewise, a gentleman is never offended by non-responses, follows, or no comments. It is, however, courteous to respond when you can on social media.

- Treat social media inboxes like email with a bit more flexibility on timeline for responding. If someone really needs to contact you, they know how to do it.

- Although we live in a society of "freedom of speech," a gentleman never makes comments to deliberately offend others, especially in the areas of race, religion, gender, politics or sexual orientation.

- Everyone does not need to know your whole life. Be interesting, but let people want to know more about the gentleman you are.

- Flirting on social media can be fun when done correctly, but never use it as your only way of communication. A gentleman uses more intimate means of communication if he wants to be taken seriously.

- Use social media to stay connected and for the quick "Hi, hello, thank you and what's up," rather than your only means of communication.

Ferrera Fresh Tip: Learn and study social media, if you choose to. It is not just a child's game, but can be a means of meeting and building stronger relationships if used correctly.

Hand-Written Communication

With technology being so prominent today, hand-written communication can be aberrant. However, the perfect gentleman knows that this can be greatly appreciated in a world where it is not often used. The best time to use a hand-written message is for comfort, care, or when you want someone to have a visible message to refer to since emails can be easily overlooked or opened and deleted. A thank-you card is a nice gesture after a business meeting or a hand-written message when someone is sick or mourning. A few things to remember in hand-written communication are:

* Be sincere. Although, this will get you points in almost any relationship, do not use it to suck up. People appreciate honesty.

* Send it within two to three days of the interaction. If you forget, you may want to make a simple phone call or leave a brief voicemail message. Do not apologize for not sending something because you really do not *have* to; it is just polite to do.

* It is also best to write the date on a hand-written message as well.

* If you are able to call to someone who is sick or mourning, do so. Note, however, that some people prefer privacy or silence during a difficult time.

* Know the person and respond accordingly. It is also okay to ask someone close to the person, whether calling or writing is best.

* Be as neat as possible when writing. It is okay if you do not have perfect handwriting. The person will still appreciate that you took time to handwrite the note. You can also have someone write or type it for you, but you still should sign it.

- Insert cards into the envelope with the front of the card facing the outside flap so the card is ready to be read when taken out. Insert the folded side at the bottom if the card has money or anything else that can slide out when the card is removed.

- If someone sends you a card, make sure you read it. That way, you can respond accordingly if they ask if you received it.

- The time frame for keeping greeting cards is completely up to you. It is appropriate to keep Christmas cards, sympathy cards, or special occasion cards in a safe place for however long or short you choose. It may be nice to refer to the sender's kind words in the future.

Ferrera Fresh Tip: Women enjoy when a man takes time and handwrites a message. Try it and use it to your advantage, often.

At a Mixer

Make sure you "mix," meaning socialize with others. Although it may be uncomfortable at first, remember to talk to a variety of people. This is how new relationships can be formed and others can enjoy your presence on a business and leisure level. If you are not in the mood to mix and mingle, simply stay home or leave the event and join people when you are ready to interact. Two to four minutes is enough time for a short conversation to exchange business cards, and see if you would like to further communicate. If you feel the need to, you can definitely hold longer conversations if you choose. The business portion of networking is not done in a few minutes at an event. It is done afterwards, in your follow-up and your regular communication with those people.

> *Ferrera Fresh Tip:* Do not keep your cell phone glued to your ears at social events as this is a time for others to embrace your gentlemanly grace.

At a Club or Bar

A gentleman is always alert and aware of his surroundings at a party, club or bar. Scope out the people around you and the environment you are in. Then order your beverage or food choices and begin enjoying the night. Notice the people you need to talk to, relax and enjoy!

> *Ferrera Fresh Tip:* Practice to eat and drink food and beverages with your left hand. This will allow your right hand to be free and clean for shaking hands or meeting people.

While Dining

The perfect gentleman knows never to talk with food in his mouth. Finish chewing and then begin to talk. The people you are eating with will wait until you finish chewing in order to hear you more clearly. Ask others questions when you see they are not eating or drinking. A good time to ask questions is when they have finished chewing, not while they are chewing or have just put food in their mouth. Now while they are talking, you chew and eat, which will make for a great dining experience in which you enjoy great conversation while having a meal.

In a Meeting

Always speak clear, crisp and confident, even if you're not completely comfortable initially. Let the other people in the room know you are there and are confident as a professional man. Please know that during meetings disagreements will occur. But it should not turn into an argument in front of others. Simply discuss it in private at a later time, if necessary.

Ferrera Fresh Tip: During a meeting the perfect gentleman never holds himself higher than others or belittles others, even when in a position of seniority.

Following Up

In business or leisure if you say you are going to follow up at a specific time, do so, no exceptions. If it simply slips your mind, contact the person as soon as possible and tell the truth so they can adjust accordingly. Without communication people just cannot respond correctly in business or leisure. If someone does not follow up with you on something of importance or something that is time sensitive, contact him or her in a respectful manner via personal email or phone. If you feel he or she is avoiding you, reevaluate the relationship. The person may indeed be avoiding you or simply has a busy schedule.

Mishear Someone

When you mishear or are unclear of what someone has said, ask them to repeat it. Try saying, "Excuse me," or "I did not hear you," or "Please come again." If you mishear people too often, you may need to work on your listening skills or you may have a hearing impairment and need to see a doctor.

Correcting Someone

When someone says a word wrong or uses it incorrectly, you should use the same word correctly when the opportunity arises. Hopefully they will use the word correct the next time. If a word continues to be used wrong, and you know the person well, correct them in private by saying, "I notice you say…. The correct way is…" The same applies to emails, and text messages if you notice spelling typos. Try to use the word yourself by correctly typing it when you reply. You will be surprised how people will notice and make changes in future use.

> *Ferrera Fresh Tip*: When correcting someone, soften the conversation a bit by saying something positive to them when you are finished, even if it has nothing to do with the correction.

Correcting a Name

If someone mispronounces your name, it is best to correct them on the spot at the first mistake so it is fresh in their mind. Do not be upset or frown. Kindly reply with "It is… (say the name correctly)." If they ask you to clarify, please do. If you mess up a name, apologize and ask the correct way. Then repeat it back to them correctly. This allows you to use it again for remembrance and clarify you are saying it properly.

Remembering Names

When meeting various people at an event, it is often difficult to remember names. If you forget, it is okay to ask, but make a conscious effort to remember. A great way to remember is to relate their name with someone or something you are familiar with. For example, if someone says, "Hello my name is Orville." You may want to connect this person's face with Orville Redenbacher Popcorn. Another example could be, "Hi my name is Patricia." Now you can *think* "my mom's name is Patricia" or "I have a good friend named Patricia." This is not to say that the person you are meeting looks like the person or object, but you are simply associating their name with something familiar. Then once you begin to know or see the person, you will remember their name naturally. It does take practice, but it is a great tip for you to use to remember names.

Introductions

This is a great way to connect people and build relationships. More than having the "proper" introduction, it is just nice to introduce people who do not know one another so that it is not awkward. Be confident in your introductions and know that all communication skills apply.

* It is also good to use the person's title, unless they have asked you not to.

* When introducing one person to another, state your relationship to the person, even if it is a person you have just met. This will allow them to start their own conversation.

* In business introduce a less prominent person to more prominent, no matter male or female.

    For example: "Dr. Strong, I would like you to meet my friend Jeff. Jeff, *this is* Dr. Mary Strong (then) Dr. Strong, this is Jeff."

* With clients or prospective clients, introduce your boss or coworkers to them. You are trying to win or keep

their business and they hold the highest stature at that time.

>For example: "Mr. Williams, meet one of our newest clients, Mr. Johnson…"

♦ Introduce all people to elders.

>For example: "Jennifer this is my grandfather, Gregory Sr."

♦ Introduce one person to a group, then the group to the one person.

>For example: "John *this is* Shawn, Mike and Brenda. Everyone this is John Wright."

♦ In social settings, ladies hold the highest stature. Therefore, introduce gentlemen to ladies.

>For example: "Jeff, this is Mary. (then) Mary, this is Jeff…"

Speaking with Family

When speaking with family members always be respectful to elders and be prepared to listen if they talk more than you need to hear. Be mindful that as men, it is in our nature to solve problems or have a solution when someone shares information. However, there are times in communication when we need to just listen. This is also important when dealing with women, but we will talk more about that later in the chapter dedicated to being the perfect gentleman with ladies.

Ferrera Fresh Tip: Take note of what works for you when introducing people and use your communication skills with confidence.

Awkward Settings

When interacting in awkward settings like airplanes, in a line, a bus, train, elevator or other public places, be respectful to other people's space. Smiling and moving with confidence as the perfect gentleman will naturally attract people to you. It is okay to say, "Hello, how are you?" in a short thirty-second dialogue. Just remember, never invade the space of someone else. Some people just don't want to be bothered for some reason or another. Recognize it and move on. But if a conversation dawns, carry on with the guides provided in this chapter.

On First Impression

Be yourself. With the guides in this book, the perfect gentleman never has a problem making a good first impression. Besides, if you are not genuine in your communication, people will *eventually* see through the fake, phony fluff and you will see it in other people too. If you think you have made a bad first impression, do not talk about it with the person immediately. Try to build on the relationship so the person can see the powerful gentleman you can be by interacting with them. If someone thinks you have been blatantly rude, apologize and move on. Don't dwell on it.

Greetings and Shaking Hands

♦ Shake hands firm with all business professionals. Let them know you are there and that you are a confident man.

♦ The fancy handshakes you have with close friends and relatives should be ditched in business settings. Yes, you can be more casual with fancy handshakes, grips, or hugs when business is complete, but always keep your cool in a business setting.

♦ When shaking hands with ladies in business, it is okay to extend your hand to ladies in the United States. Women are business professionals as well, and it could be insulting to some if you do not greet them as you would another professional. This is why it is fine to shake hands with ladies.

♦ If you are traveling, remember to research proper etiquette for greeting others prior to your travels.

Ferrera Fresh Tip: When visiting other countries or cultures, be mindful of how to greet both males and females. It is a good idea to ask others who may know since there may be cultural differences regarding how people greet one another.

Great Ice-Breaking Questions:

+ "How do you know the host of the party?"

+ "How did you hear about the event?"

+ "Do you live, work or leisure near this city?"

+ "How long have you been a member of the club?"

+ "I haven't talked to you in a while. What good things are going on?"

Always remember these question are to help lead into a conversation. Once you hear their answer, see how you can respond in some relation to carry on the conversation. As the perfect gentleman, practice your listening skills and learn what type of questions can lead you into further conversation. Remember to change words in these ice breaker questions as it pertains to the event or phone call etc.

> *Ferrera Fresh Tip:* A great way to exit a conversation is to introduce the person to another person, so they can begin talking and you can excuse yourself from the conversation.

Great Exit Conversation Statements:

+ "Great chatting with you. Please let me say hello to some other friends."

+ "Let's exchange contact information or business cards, and maybe we can talk again soon."

+ "Please excuse me for a moment. I'm going to the (insert a different location) "

The Communication Recap

When communicating, as the perfect gentleman, be graceful, kind and respectful. Although interactions might be short, they can leave lasting impressions. As the perfect gentleman, you always want to leave a positive impression in any type of interaction. Remember that eye contact, a nice volume in your voice and good posture will convey confidence to the people you communicate with. People enjoy communicating with others who are confident in their communication skills. Now, as you are confident in your communication, embrace the opportunity to interactg with others. After all, you are the perfect gentleman and they will surely enjoy communicating with you.

5
The Perfect Gentleman
Handles Business

Often business environments are thought of as places where everything should be proper, boring and uptight. However, when conducting business you *can be* cordial and cool at the same time. Cordiality, respect, and consideration for others apply when conducting business just as much as they do in social interactions. In this section of The PGPG you will find tips and ideas on being a respectful business professional, while still keeping your swagger as the perfect gentleman.

Ferrera Fresh Tip: You are a representation of your company more than you can imagine. Always be at your best to present yourself and your company in the best way possible.

Relationships

The relationships you form in business are far more important than the products you sell or the services you provide. There is always someone else who can provide the product or service you do. They may not be as good, but they can do it. As the perfect gentleman, focus on building relationships with your clients, customers and the people around you. When building relationships the perfect gentleman knows:

- *Listen* and find out what people need, want and expect you to provide and how they want it provided. Each person may have their individual needs and as the perfect gentleman, do your best to address them.

- Birthdays, anniversaries, and holidays are great ways to build on the relationship between the perfect gentleman and business patrons.

- A simple phone call, greeting card or message with no business agenda behind it will be appreciated by the people you conduct business with on a consistent basis.

- Social media (i.e., Facebook, Twitter and Linkedin) can be your friend in business. By learning what your clients, customers and business associates enjoy can allow for personalized gift giving and can help build upon a growing relationship.

- Be genuine in your relationship building. Yes, it will eventually bring you more business, but the relationship you have with people is more important than just another business transaction.

> *Ferrera Fresh Tip*: Remember that people don't buy products or services. They buy people to provide the products or services.

Interviews

The job interview is one of the most important direct interactions you will have with a potential organization or company and you should be at your absolute best. Courtesy and politeness are musts, and should be habits for you as the perfect gentleman. Your charisma as the perfect gentleman will make others, including business professionals, be interested in you and your affairs. A few things to remember on the first interview or during promotional interviews are:

* Be on time to the appointment, meaning arrive ten minutes early. Yes, you may have to wait a bit, but that is better than arriving in a rush.

* Being on time or early will also give you time to meet the receptionist. Get him or her to like you. Smile, shake hands, and be engaging within the first few minutes. Many employers ask their receptionist's opinion on what they thought of you, which can have an impact on the hiring decision.

* In the interview, all gentleman communication skills apply. Posture, tone, motions, and eye contact are all huge in making a powerful first impression. (Reference previous chapter as needed.)

* Answer the questions they ask and only offer new information that you think will be helpful to get the position. Do not just talk to show that you speak well. Listen and respond attentively if you are sincere about seeking the position.

- Be prepared to ask at least one question. It shows you are interested in the position and you have done personal research prior to the interview. Try not to say, "No, I don't have any questions," if they ask you.

- I suggest asking a positive question such as, "I notice you are expanding your office locations to the east coast. When are you planning to open them?" This type of question holds more weight than "I notice your sales are down 30%. What are you going to do about that?"

- If the interviewer does not ask you if you have any questions pertaining to the job, do not ask. You may have the opportunity to ask at another time or in another interview.

- If the company states they will contact you, you can ask when you should expect to hear from them so you can plan accordingly. And yes, you can contact them by phone one to two business days after the time stated if they do not call you.

- Remember to never be rude or *show* that you are upset if you do not get a position. You never want to burn any bridges in business since you might come across the same people at a later date.

> *Ferrera Fresh Tip*: Send a thank-you card on the day of the interview to the person who interviewed you. It's a nice gesture and it might even help you get the position.

Interviews & What to Wear

Regardless of how well your resume looks or how many qualifications you have listed, employers will still be assessing the person you are. Even during phone interviews, the interviewers are evaluating how you communicate. In addition, when you have an in-person interview, they are also assessing your presentation and attire. The human mind by habit is trained to generate thoughts about everything on first sight. By sight we choose who we talk to, the food we eat, and the books we read. We judge all these things on sight within a few seconds. You have even done it on the book you're reading right now. This is also exactly what the job interviewer is doing to you as well. Yes, image is important on a job interview because employers want you to represent them well, if they decide to hire you. As the perfect gentleman here are a few things to remember when dressing for interviews:

◆ Whatever job you are seeking, dress one notch higher than the position you are seeking. If daily dress for the company is a polo shirt and pants, choose to wear a dress shirt, tie and slacks. If daily dress is slacks and a dress shirt, then add a tie or go for the full suit and tie.

◆ Although you may have a three-piece suit, ditch the vest on the first interview. A three-piece suit can be too powerful. Since most men do not wear three-piece suits every day, you do not want to give the image of being superior when you are the one seeking the job. Yes, once you have the position, gradually transition into your complete style of the three-piece suit, if you choose.

- When choosing shirt color it is best to be simple and then stylish. Whites and light blues are always classic, cool and professional.

- Checks, stripes and patterns are fine to wear during interviews. Just make sure they are not too bold. Any stripe wider than half the width of a shirt button is too bold. You want the interviewer to focus on you, not on how fancy your clothes are.

- Avoid dark shirts for interviews. Colors like black, dark brown, navy, or forest green are not as pleasing to the eye. Lighter colors are more welcoming during interviews.

- Ties are great in base colors of navy blue, gray, or lavender. They also are great with different colors and designs in them. Again, choose light colors that are more welcoming to the eye.

- In the business suit, opt for navy blue or gray on the first interview. These suit colors are welcoming, classic, cool and professional.

- Pinstripes are fine, but not too bold. Avoid the plaid suit during first interviews. This pattern is too busy for an interview. You can wear plaid once you have the job, but plaid can be distracting on first interactions.

- If you only have certain items in certain colors, wear the items you have with confidence.

* For phone interviews I would even recommend dressing professional to some extent because it will help you get in professional mode. A polo shirt at the least is good enough to get you in the right mindset.

* For second interviews, use the same dress etiquette as first interviews. On third or promotion interviews, the company already knows you, so *dress up* with your personal style.

Ferrera Fresh Tip: Looking good on job interviews doesn't mean you have to spend a lot of money, but it does mean you need to be neat, clean and organized.

The First Day of Work

Be confident. The first day is when everyone is watching you. General greetings, hellos and introductions are appropriate. Share with them what you want them to know about you and nothing more. You are observing them just as they are observing you. Do not over do it by being overly "cheery" and "buddy-buddy" with everyone. Ease your way into the environment and display yourself as the perfect gentleman.

Ferrera Fresh Tip: Whether it's your first day on a job or your tenth year with a company, never be afraid to ask for help. Our individual knowledge and talents should be used to help others.

Office Etiquette

In business the perfect gentleman completes everything he has committed to. That is not to say you cannot make changes in business, but always follow through. From the simplest new job agreement to the end of a major business transaction, the perfect gentleman is honest in his actions.

In the working world there are some people who are nicer than others, have different ways of interacting, eating, communicating and the list of differences can go on. Remember to be respectful and considerate of others. As the perfect gentleman here are a few tips so that your business etiquette is just as sharp as in any other interaction:

- If you walk into a room and someone else is there before you, you are the one that initiates the hello. You are entering their space.

- Please, thank you, good morning, good-bye and general greetings are standard procedure for the perfect gentleman.

- If you borrow or use someone's item or a community item, always return it. Ask before using it, even when it is a simple pen or notepad. If you forget to return something, do so the moment you notice.

- Radio, music, internet sites, short videos or movies and all distractions we have at work should be minimized and controlled. Be mindful not to disturb others with loud or offensive material. You are there to work, not leisure.

- Know your areas or personal space as well as others' personal space. Likewise, know community areas in your workplace and be even more respectful in these areas.

- Mind your own business. Just because something is in an open area does not mean you look at, touch, listen in or see what's going on.

- All sensitive information for your clients and customers should be protected and kept confidential, no matter how comfortable you are with your office.

- Know your environment. A hard hat work environment is different from a twenty-five story bank building, so act accordingly to your values and environment. Know what language, activities, conversation, dress and so on are appropriate for your workplace.

- When taking messages for people, be as detailed as possible. Try to always get a number so the person receiving the message does not have to look it up. And, remember to deliver the message since we sometimes forget.

- If someone around you is sick, take your sickness prevention vitamins so that you do not get sick. If a person's sickness is a distraction after a while, you may want to suggest to him or her that, "You may want to go home." Most of the time it is better for everyone, especially the person who is sick.

- Never burn bridges when leaving any work position. You might encounter former coworkers and bosses again and you never want to leave an ill feeling that may hamper you in the future.

- Finally, workplace jealousy exists too. Some will hate to see you do well and get promotions. The best thing to do is accept it and embrace it. Do not be rude or stoop to their level or entertain their foolishness.

Ferrera Fresh Tip: The office or workplace is just another place for you to display your grace as the perfect gentleman. Keep your confidence and swagger as you would in any other environment.

Leaving a Company

Leaving a job or a company might be exciting or it might not. The relationships you have made will determine how you feel. Either way, never behave in a rude or disrespectful manner to anyone, no matter how bad or awkward they've made you feel during your time there. Leaving a job or company is not always a bad thing since it may be that you are moving on to better opportunities. Regardless, here are a few things to remember to make your exit as the perfect gentleman:

◆ Being respectful is the most important. Respectful includes informing managers and presidents that you will be leaving the company at a particular time. Note: giving a two-week notice is standard.

◆ If they ask your reason for leaving, be genuine. This can help them assess if they are doing an adequate job in providing new opportunities for their employees or if they can do better as a company.

◆ If there are any ill feelings toward or from a particular person, simply make your exit. You do not have to make a closing statement or give them "a piece of your mind." As the perfect gentleman, just move on.

◆ You can tell the people what you will be doing if you want. However, if you rather not share information with them, just state that you will be exploring new options. How much information you reveal is completely up to you.

Ferrera Fresh Tip: In business and leisure the perfect gentleman makes a graceful exit. Even when gone, a gentleman's grace will still be remembered.

Laying Someone Off

If you are the boss, there may be times when you must lay someone off, terminate an employee, downsize or eliminate a position. Being respectful still applies. A few tips to remember in this situation are:

* Use the right protocol that your firm has in place for layoffs.

* Keep discussions private. Never lay someone off in public, even if they deserve it and are not so nice to you as the boss.

* Inform the person about your reasons for making the decision. As long as the reason is not against the law, it is best to let them know truthfully. Sharing the reason will let them know if there is something they can do better in the future.

* Only the leaders, managers and decision makers of the company *need* to know about plans for layoffs. If other employees ask about a particular person or the layoff of others, you can disclose if you wish, but be truthful and respectful.

* Sincerely think about the decisions you choose to make and be confident in them. You are the boss.

Referrals

As the perfect gentleman in business, people will want to know and be around the people you know to expand their network. Likewise, you will want to meet other business professionals to expand your network. As mentioned before, the relationship is the most important aspect of the business world. People do business with people they know, like and genuinely trust. In business the perfect gentleman knows the proper way to give and receive referrals.

Giving Referrals

* Naturally, when you give respectable referrals to other business professionals, other people will give referrals to you.

* When giving a referral, never expect anything in return— no money, compensation, gifts or anything. If someone offers something to you, accept it, but do not initially *expect* anything.

* It is fine for a gentleman to give another person's information to someone else when you know both individuals well enough and the person receiving the referral can use your name when contacting.

* If someone has asked you not to share particular information with others, respect their wishes without hesitation.

* Share with the person receiving the referral, a name, how you know the person, the best time to contact and method of contact preferred as well as how they might be able to work together. The completion of business is still the responsibility of both parties, not yours.

* If you would like a follow-up on the relationship, it is your choice. However, when giving referrals, you are only responsible for assisting with a detailed introduction.

- It is also best to contact the people you are referring. Inform them that the specific person you referred to them will contact them, and they should expect the contact. It's just courteous.

> *Ferrera Fresh Tip*: Be confident in giving, receiving, and contacting referrals. Your confidence will make others feel comfortable in doing business with you and potentially can lead to more business.

Receiving Referrals

- Always thank the person that has given you the referrals, even if you do not know the type of business that will or will not be generated.

- Just as when giving referrals, you do not *have* to compensate people for giving you referrals. You can choose to give something if you would like. It is a nice gesture and may get you more referrals, but it is completely your choice.

- Make sure to follow up with the people you were referred to. Many people miss opportunities because they forget to follow up promptly. If you cannot do it, hire an assistant to contact them for you.

- Contacting referrals within two to five days after you receive the referral is best so that it is fresh in your mind, unless you were given other instructions as to when to contact them. If you forget, contact them as soon as you can.

- Respect the person you are referred to, even though you do not know them yet. Respect their time and availability, when they can and cannot communicate, and then proceed with business as usual.

- When you contact the referral, it is best to share your name, how you were referred to them, your company name and the reason you are contacting. The referring person alone may be enough to carry a conversation.

> *Ferrera Fresh Tip:* When contacting CEOs and people at the forefront of companies, you may have to contact them at awkward hours. Most of them are available before the other employees arrive and when most employees have left.

Meetings, Seating, and Presentations

Unless specified, there is no seating chart for meetings or presentations. The only unspoken rule is that the person conducting the meeting should be at the head of the table or in the place where everyone can see them. This rule also applies to business meals. A few things to remember as the perfect gentleman:

- Be respectful of those around you. Do not block the view of anyone, disrupt their space or any other business proceedings.

- If you need to step out of a meeting or presentation, the best time to do so is when the speaker has a break, a pause, or a transition of topics.

- A great time to exit is when the speaker begins to write on a board, changes a presentation slide, or at a point that causes a pause in the presentation. If that never happens, just calmly excuse yourself.

- Minimize as much noise or disturbance to other people on your way out and when returning.

- Minimize text messages, emails, and mobile activity when in group settings. It's very distracting and disrespectful to the speaker.

- Unless you are expecting an important call that you must take, turn your phone on complete silent. When your phone is on vibrate, it can be just as distracting to the people around you as a full ring. You can return calls and messages when you are done.

- If you ever need to leave a one-on-one or small meeting with five or less people, just ask to be excused.

Ferrera Fresh Tip: If your phone goes off in a meeting by accident, try to simply stop the ringer first. Don't try to run out of the building to stop the noise as that may only cause more of a disturbance.

Speaking in Front of Groups

- When speaking in front of a group of 100 people or less, make direct eye contact with some of your listeners and use face-to-face communication guidelines.

- With larger groups of people, you may want to move around to engage your audience. Speak loud, bold, and with confidence. A gentleman demands focus no matter the group size.

Planning Before Events or Meetings

The perfect gentleman plans to keep and attend all business meetings, appointments and social engagements once they have been confirmed. There is no *need* to confirm an appointment with you, the perfect gentleman, because the appointments you set, you keep. If you prefer to confirm an appointment, it should be done by phone or email at least 24 hours or more in advance. Prior to any engagement, the perfect gentleman knows what the attire is, who else may be in attendance, and other important aspects such as food to be served, parking instructions and related costs. Not only is your time important, but as a gentleman, you are considerate of the time and planning of others as well.

> *Ferrera Fresh Tip:* There is no need to reconfirm an appointment you've already confirmed; that's just silly.

Be On Time

The perfect gentleman should always be on time. Your tardiness can hold up other engagements and may cause you to miss out on business deals. Being late can also cause you to have to play catch up for the rest of the day. Your tardiness can create a domino effect and cause you to be late to every subsequent appointment, which is completely unacceptable. When an appointment is set in business, plan to arrive about 15-20 minutes early. This does not always mean that you walk in to the meeting early. Your appointment may not be ready for you to arrive early and may have other appointments or things to do before you arrive at the time set.

I have found that by planning to arrive 15-20 minutes early allows some time for error such as the correction of wrong directions on a map, commute traffic, bus or train delays, construction detours or other things that could cause you to be late. The 15-20 minutes you have allotted can cause you to still be on time despite other factors.

I am Early

Since you have planned to be early to your appointments, it will become a habit and you may have down time before an appointment. No one wants to be sitting, waiting, and doing nothing, so this is a great time to follow up on minor tasks of the day. Grab your mobile device and follow up on a few emails, return or make a short call you have not had time for. Keep a book handy to read a few pages, or simply bring out your Perfect Gentleman's Pocket Guide for a light refresher. You can also take a moment to give a midday call to a special lady. She will appreciate that you took time out of your busy schedule. Alternatively, if your appointment is with someone you know, it is okay to call and say, "I'm running a little ahead of schedule, would you mind if I arrive a little early?" Then act accordingly.

I am Going to be Late

In some situations, life just happens and it will cause us to be late. Just do not make it a habit. When you know you will be late, it is best to call and let the other involved parties know your situation and when you will be there. Something like, "<u>NAME</u>, I'm in traffic and I will be a little behind schedule. I will be there in _____ minutes." Three things for the perfect gentleman to remember when you are late are:

1. Call the moment you realize you are going to be late, not two minutes before the appointment time.

2. Provide a real time that you will arrive. Do not say you will be there in 10 minutes when it's really going to be 30. Again, be considerate of the other person's time.

3. Be safe. Rushing can cause accidents and it is better to be late, rather than not arrive safely.

> *Ferrera Fresh Tip*: Text messages when late are okay only if you know the person cannot speak at that moment. A phone call is more effective because you may get to talk to the person, which will allow them to plan accordingly.

I am Already Late

Accept it. Do not beat yourself up about being late. Yes, correct yourself and do not make it a habit, because being late is not the end of the world. The most important thing is that you arrive in one piece. It is better to be late and prepared when you arrive, than late and unprepared because you were rushing. Make sure to call and inform the person. Try something like "I realize that your event starts at eight o'clock and it's eight-forty now. Is it still okay if I arrive in a bit?" Then respond accordingly. If the person you are contacting is unable to answer, the perfect gentleman mindset must go into play and you make a decision. Even if you show up for the end or middle, you did make an attempt and explain your situation. Remember, if being late is regular for you, it will not be well received and you may want to plan better.

I am Here Now

If you arrive late to an appointment, business event or social activity, accept it and move on. If you are entering a session that has already begun, enter with minimal noise to avoid disturbing others or proceedings already in progress. Now that you have arrived, apologize when you have a chance and move on. There is no need for three and four, "I'm sorry for being late" comments. It happens to the best of us. Also, there is no need to give any full-length story as to why you are late. There is no excuse and it really doesn't matter. The only reason would be if there is a funny little story that you think others may enjoy.

I Cannot Make It

If you are unable to attend a confirmed meeting time, a phone call must be made. A text message is not an option here. A phone call should be made the moment you realize you cannot make it, not the day of ten minutes before. A last-minute call is only acceptable in the event of an emergency. If you know that you cannot make it on Tuesday and your appointment is set for Friday, call on Tuesday or as soon as possible. Your appointment will be able to adjust their schedule and better coordinate their calendar.

Your Appointment is Early, Late or Cannot Make It

In this situation you are on the receiving end so what do you do? You may have to recommend this book to them if they do not act appropriately. Nonetheless, in all situations we must forgive. If it happens once, nothing needs to be said. If it does happen more than once, you can share with the person how you feel, but never be rude. They may already feel uncomfortable that the situation has occurred and there is no need for you to make it worse. If it just continuously happens, you may want to reconsider your association and move on. If you had a specific start and end time for the appointment and the person is late, you do not have to allow additional time. It is your choice and you can simply end the meeting as planned to stay on track with the rest of your schedule.

> *Ferrera Fresh Tip:* What you plan for is what you will receive and what you give to others is what you will receive in return. Be considerate and respectful of other people's time.

Voicemail

Leaving a proper voicemail or greeting is so important because first impressions may not always be in person. A voicemail may be the first interaction you have with others. Therefore, you want your voice to be sharp, clear and crisp. Your voicemail greeting should be welcoming and inviting to callers, making them want to leave you a message. Give instructions on what information you would like them to leave such as name, phone number and the best time to return the call. Also, try using the words "*Please,* leave a message." It will cause people to actually leave more messages, making it easier for you to get back to people.

Business Card

Simply put, your business card should be a reflection of you. The image you want to portray to others should be displayed on your card. Of course, your name, company name and contact information is essential. You should try to have some type of physical address, even if you do not have a physical location. Your address will subconsciously create an image in the other person's mind of where you are located, even if it is just for postal mail purposes, but it is your choice. Talk with graphic designers or the person making your cards. They are the professionals and can help you with the presentation. Pictures, images and logos are fine too and the choice is up to you. Regardless, the perfect gentleman always has business cards ready and available to hand out if he wants to be contacted.

Ferrera Fresh Tip: Sometimes less is more. The simple business card can give an image of prestige and professionalism, which is never wrong for the perfect gentleman in business.

Business Lunch

Depending on how close you are with the other people you work with, a lunch break can be a great time to build on relationships and assist others. If you are heading to lunch, you may want to invite someone or offer to bring something back to make their day easier. A few ideas to make your business lunch most effective are:

◆ Lunch breaks do not have to be long, but if you choose a long lunch, that is fine. Just be considerate of other people's time during business lunches.

◆ Opt for lighter meals when out for lunch so that when you are back to work you are not tired or sleepy because of heavy food.

- If you are in a group work environment and someone asks you to bring something back for them, do it. Just as well, if you are comfortable with others, you can ask for the favor of bringing something back for you.

- You do not always have to treat people when they ask you to bring them something, but please do if you are able.

- If someone is treating you to a business lunch, respectfully enjoy. There is no need to offer to pay, add a portion or anything; accept the treat.

- If you are planning the business lunch, make sure the arrangements on paying are known so there is no confusion.

- Be conscious that they are treating you and order something that you would treat yourself to if you were paying.

- As the perfect gentleman in business, always take mental notes of who drove last, who picked up the tab last and other such things in order to rotate without leaving the burden always on one person.

- If you are in a lunchroom where others may be, keep your area neat and clean. Hopefully, it will cause others to do the same. Your dishes, cups, trash or anything else should not be left in a sink or lying around. Not only is it nasty, but it is distracting to others.

As the perfect gentleman in business, remember that the business arena is simply another place for you to display your grace and character while not having to be uptight or nerdy. Also, recognize the difference between being productive in business and being busy. You are productive when you are moving toward completing tasks and obtaining results. This is important because just as the perfect gentleman works hard in business, he also must partake in leisure. Although it is easy to get caught up in doing business, never forget to add the element of *leisure*, which the perfect gentleman does oh so well.

6
The Perfect Gentleman
Embraces Entertainment & Leisure

A s the perfect gentleman, people will be delighted to be in your presence. This means you will be invited to numerous leisure and entertainment events. In this section of The PGPG you will find tips on your conduct, how to accept or decline an invite, how to plan for travel, and how to choose appropriate attire for all occasions. It is important to remember that you do not have to attend everything and, quite frankly, you can't. A perfect gentleman is busy taking care of business but does indulge in a pleasant social gathering every now and again.

Invitations
Invitations to social events may come in different forms. Invites may be verbal, by postal mail, email, social media

invite, text message, and the list can go on. When viewing and responding to invitations the perfect gentleman always knows:

- To respond by the same means the invitation is received or as stated in the invitation. If the invite is by phone call, call the person back on the phone with your response. If the invite is in email form, respond via email. If the invitation is in one form and it asks you to respond in a particular way, do so.

- An invitation is not open to you and guests. Guests are welcome only if the invitation states so. If you would like to bring a guest, it is best to ask if you can.

- If you receive an invitation that requests a response of attendance by a specific date, always comply with that date.

- If you forget to respond or you receive an invitation late, contact the host by phone and inform him or her on your attendance. If you forgot to respond by the date, be willing to accept the fact that reservations might already be filled and you will be unable to attend.

- Some invitations ask for a response as "regrets only." This means you only need to reply if you cannot attend.

- The perfect gentleman does not wait until something better comes up to confirm or decline an invitation. However, it is okay to wait and confirm if an existing calendar event may conflict.

- If you are hosting an event such as a social, a house party, birthday party, or other such gatherings, the invitations should be sent out at least thirty days in advance so that guests can plan.

- Invitations for large events such as a weddings, momentous birthdays or occasions, anything that requires travel and other such events should be sent out at least three to six months in advance.

> *Ferrera Fresh Tip:* It is nice to know what the letters R.S.V.P. actually mean. Yes, it does mean that you need to respond regarding your attendance. But the letters stand for Répondez S'il Vous Plaît, which is French for "Please Respond." Now you know.

Turning Down an Invitation

- When turning down an invitation, respond as soon as you know you cannot make it.

- If you have to turn down an invitation you have already accepted and confirmed, it is best to do it with a phone call or some form of direct contact.

- There is no need for long explanations as to why you cannot attend. Give your reason and move on.

- There is also no need to lie. Apologize that you cannot make it, but there is no need to give promises to attend their next event or anything else.

- If someone is bugging you to attend an event, inform him or her of your attendance and do not let it bother you.

- The perfect gentleman knows that it is completely okay not to attend an event. The perfect gentleman is respectful and selective about the events he attends.

- The perfect gentleman, that hosts an event, never forces, manipulates or pressures anyone to attend. Simply give the invitation and encourage people to come respectfully.

Arriving to Events

When arriving to a leisure event at someone's home the perfect gentleman knows:

- Arrive on time, but do your best not to be the first one to arrive. "How is this possible?" you ask. "On time" to a social event is any time approximately thirty to sixty minutes after the start time. Most ladies will arrive before then and you are fine.

- It might even be kind to ask prior to the event, "What is the best time to arrive?"

- It is a nice gesture to bring a gift to the person's home on the *first* visit or if you haven't visited in more than 12 months. Gifts do not have to be expensive; sometimes a thank-you card is enough. Cookies, chocolate, or a plant are nice gift ideas as well. Know the person you are visiting and bless them accordingly.

- It is respectful to remove shoes *only* if the host asks you to. However, if you prefer not to take off your shoes, you can ask if it is okay to leave them on and respond accordingly. Just take a mental note for your future visits.

Ferrera Fresh Tip: When attending social events that have waiting lines, try to build relationships with the people that can provide direct access on future visits.

Arrive Exactly on Time or Early for:

♦ Weddings, movies, theatres, plays, organized dinners, places where you have reservations, dates with a lady, vacation travel plans, kids' sporting events or birthday parties, golf, graduations, boat parties, award ceremonies, funerals, political events or any event that demands being on time not as a suggestion.

Arrive within the Hour for:

♦ Clubs, bars, fight night, mixers, bachelor parties, or simple hangouts.

♦ If the guest list for the hangout is less than five people, make sure you know when everyone is expected to arrive. That way no one person feels uncomfortable. Late etiquette applies as stated in Chapter 5 *(page136)*.

Assigned Seating Events

When attending any event where seats are assigned such as a baseball or basketball game, concerts or theatre plays, always sit in your assigned seat and respect others around you. There will be occasions when swapping seats may be better for convenience, which is okay, but be considerate of others. At assigned seating events, the perfect gentleman knows:

♦ Be aware of those already seated. If you show up to an event and need to pass people already seated, enter the aisle facing them so you do not put your butt in their face as you pass.

- Try to make beer and snack runs when others are already standing or during an intermission.

Ferrera Fresh Tip: Take care of unimportant phone calls and other miscellaneous activities before or after your event. You are there to participate in the event. Enjoy.

Reading

The perfect gentleman reads books and does not claim to have read a book he hasn't. It is perfectly okay not to have read a book everyone may be talking about. There is no way we can read every book, but it is appropriate for the perfect gentleman to pick up a good book every now and again. The same applies with newspapers, movies, television shows, music and so forth. Never falsely claim to have read or watched something. As the perfect gentleman it is good to know a bit about current events that are happening and what is popular at the time so you can carry on good conversations at random with others.

Sporting Events and Activities

At sporting events, be a fan. The perfect gentleman can still high-five, chest bump and wear a hat backwards. Some humorous taunting is fine as well, but never deliberately be rude to another fan. Tone the taunting down and be respectful at children's events. The kids are watching and hearing you and will learn from your actions.

Fishing, boating, poker, dominos, chess or any other so-called "man" events are more enjoyable with good company. Treat them just as any other invitation and act accordingly. Biking, hiking, skateboarding and more are to be done only in the appropriate areas. Although it may be hard to resist biking or skateboarding in a private area, and you may get away with it, you must stop if ever asked to do so by an official.

Golf

Golfing is a social event to partake in only if you like it. In addition to just having a good time with your golf group, it is a good way to meet other business professionals. It is much easier to have a conversation on the golf course than during a football game because it is more quiet. A few things to remember when golfing are:

♦ ALWAYS be on time for golf. Whatever time you have set as your *tee time*, be there at least twenty minutes before. You can throw off the whole day or even be skipped if you are late.

♦ Know the rules of golf. If you don't know, read up on it or ask others you know for assistance.

♦ Make sure to own or rent the proper equipment required in order to be respectful to the golf course facilities.

♦ If you have a caddy, treat him or her as part of your group and tip them monetarily at the end of your round. About 10-20% of the cost of your round is a nice tip to the caddy.

♦ If you choose to go golfing regularly in a group, practice in between sessions so you can hold your own weight in the group you are with so you do not hold anyone up.

- Never cut someone from your foursome or group because he or she is not that good. This can hurt a relationship off the golf course as well. Rather than ditch them, help improve their skills.

- If someone is often late, is rude, or something of the sort, it is okay to let them go for that reason.

- Know the other unspoken rules of golf such as watch others players' golf ball and help them find it as needed, compliment good golf swings; sound off "fore" when you don't know where the ball will land. There are others, but you will learn them as you play more.

Ferrera Fresh Tip: Golf is challenging and can be very fun with other gents and ladies alike. Try golf. At least try it once.

Hosting an Event

There will come times in life when you as the perfect gentleman must host an event. Events can be held at an outside location or can take place in your home. Either way, you are the host, and you want your guests to feel as welcome as possible. If you choose to hire a host or event coordinator, let them run the show, but know it is still your event and the guests' enjoyment is still based on your cordiality. You have simply hired a coordinator to perform their talents. Whether the event is grand or a simple gathering, the perfect gentleman knows:

- Greet all or as many of your guests as possible during large events. A simple "hello, what's up, thank you for coming" is enough. However, you can chat longer if you so choose.

- Introduce guests to one another so conversations can carry on without you being present.

- You may want to leave a few people in groups without full introductions when it is a large event so they can chat amongst themselves when you are away.

- Treat your guests as much as possible to light food, cake, spirits and so forth. You are the host and gentleman and want to make the event as pleasant as possible for your guests.

- Also, remember you are not there to fill your guests up or get them drunk.

- As the host, try to eat food or snacks before your event starts, which will allow you more time to interact with your guests.

- If you have guests in your home, be prepared for your guests by always having clean dishes and glasses. There is no need to rinse off dishes or glasses just before serving something in them.

- If you prefer guests to take their shoes off in your home, it is proper to provide some sort of house shoe for guests who rather not walk around barefoot.

- If you host a full dinner party, remember to set the main dinner table properly with your best dishes or China.

- Only use glass when serving your guests beverages and try to actually *serve* them as often as possible, allowing them to enjoy themselves.

- If a dish or anything breaks at your home, accept it. It comes with the territory. Do not show your disappointment in front of your guests; just move on.

- When you have lingering guests, the perfect gentleman must accept it for a bit. If it becomes too unbearable, begin to lightly clean up and hopefully your lingering guests will get the point. Move a few glasses here and there, as you engage in wrap-up conversation.

- If the lingering continues, forget the boring stories and hints. Just politely suggest, "I'm going to call it a night. Do you have arrangements to get home?" Then respond accordingly. Call a cab, offer a room, or ask a mutual friend to accommodate them. If it is a lady, she may be giving you a hint. Again, respond accordingly and respectfully.

- After the event, thank your guests for attending your event either by postal mail, e-mail, or voice mail.

Ferrera Fresh Tip: When thanking your guests, the higher the caliber of the event the more personal the thank you should be. A written note card delivered by postal mail is the highest form of thank you.

The Perfect Gentleman Gives a Toast

The key to the perfect toast is to be short and sweet. There is no need for long, drawn out stories and jokes. You are not there to embarrass anyone with personal stories, nor do you want to bore guests with your long-winded speech. A few helpful tips when giving the perfect toast are:

- Be sincere. A great way to start is by thanking the guests who have come and thanking the host for allowing you to speak.

- Be confident in front of the group, even if you are not completely comfortable speaking.

- Share one or two sentences about how you know the host or honoree and how happy you are to attend. Say a few kind words and nothing more is *needed*.

- If you choose to elaborate, it's up to you. Just remember to be brief and be respectful.

- Try to stay within two to four minutes so as not to take up too much time or bore the guests.

- Thank the guests again for sharing the moment and close.

- Remember to raise your glass of champagne or other beverage, indicating to the guests that you are finished. Gently touch glasses with others, sip and proceed with the event.

Ferrera Fresh Tip: When giving a toast or acceptance, sometimes less is more and your humility can mean more than your words.

The Perfect Gentleman and Alcohol

The perfect gentleman can enjoy an occasional alcoholic beverage every now and again. Of course, as with anything else, drinking alcohol is a personal choice. When consuming alcohol the perfect gentleman knows:

- Drinking alcohol is only appropriate for those of legal drinking age. And a gentleman does not entice any child or someone under age to drink alcohol, even at the slightest taste.

- The perfect gentleman does not drink with the intention to get drunk! Drinking alcohol becomes inappropriate when it is abused or over consumed.

- Never drink to cover up sorrow. I know it's easier said than done, but please know it will save you heartache.

- The perfect gentleman knows that drinking is a choice and only offers to others as a polite gesture, but never assumes or pressures anyone to drink once they have declined an offer.

- Do not leave drinks unmonitored among crowds you are not familiar with. Unfortunately, everyone is not the perfect gentleman, so be alert.

- If you ever drink too much, hopefully you have friends there to help. If not, ask. It is also okay to suggest to friends to stop drinking for the moment if you feel they may have had too much. One way to do so is to change location, away from the bar or alcohol.

- It is important to note that as the perfect gentleman you are always ready and alert to help your friends in need when they consume alcohol.

- The perfect gentleman does not drink and drive. There is nothing "unmanly" about handing your car keys to a sober person to drive on your behalf. That's just wise!

- Know your body. All gents are different and consumption levels and the way we response to them will vary. Also, know what you like and don't like and know how you respond to it.

- Just as when eating, a gentleman treats others to drinks and kindly accepts drinks from others as well.

> *Ferrera Fresh Tip:* If drinking is ever a problem, accept it, and seek help in public or private. 800.729.6687 or www.ncadi.samhsa.gov

The Perfect Gentleman Attends a Dance

If attending a dance, ball, gala or any other outing where dancing is involved, the perfect gentleman should dance if asked to by a lady. If you are thinking *I don't know how to dance.* The perfect gentleman always knows a good "two step," which will get you by in almost any type of music, fast or slow.

- One way to get by if you really don't know how to dance is making a subtle joke as you walk to the dance floor by saying "You may have to show me a thing or two on the floor tonight Ms." (No name just Ms.) However, still be confident when you are with her.

- The perfect gentleman must know how to slow dance. If you do not know how, learn. Your mother, aunt, female friend or someone close to you is who you must humbly approach and ask.

- You can choose to learn the Waltz, salsa, calypso and other special dances by taking lessons, although it is not required.

> *Ferrera Fresh Tip:* If you're invited to special dances often, learn the dances in your private time. You don't want to miss out on the fun, especially with the ladies.

The Perfect Gentleman is The Perfect Escort

When escorting a lady to an event make sure to actually escort her. That means walk by her side, let her embrace your arm and walk confidently with the lady you are with. Let her know that you are there for comfort as a provider and protector throughout the night. As the perfect escort, the perfect gentleman knows:

- It is best to walk with her on your left side if you are right handed and on your right side if you are left handed. This will allow your dominant hand to be available to open doors, grab a glass of wine and cater to her.

- Since she may be wearing high heels, always allow her to hold on to you as she walks up and down stairs, over tile or any awkward walking area. Be there to brace her from any fall.

- If you are in a narrow stairway going up, walk directly behind her to watch carefully for her as she walks up. If you are going down, walk in front of her so that she can hold on to your shoulder for support.

- Do not squeeze her hand too tight, but rather let her feel as if she is in control, even though you are.

- Pull out the chair for her, offer a drink, open doors and do all the things you know the perfect gentleman does so well.

The Social Kiss

The social kiss on the cheek is a greeting the perfect gentleman happily accepts. The social kiss is nothing more than a light hug as the cheeks touch as in the motion to kiss. When a social kiss happens, do not wipe off any minor lipstick left on your cheek in front of the lady. Rather, wear it as a badge of honor for the moment and

Ferrera Fresh Tip: Gents, do not let another lady wipe lipstick off your cheek unless it is the one who kissed you. She might be flirting with you if she does, but otherwise you do it!

when you get a free moment, discreetly wipe it off with your handkerchief or tissue.

The Perfect Gentleman Travels

Ahhh, yes. Whether it is for business or pleasure the perfect gentleman is always prepared when traveling on a plane, boat, train or other mode of transportation. The most important thing in travel is to apply all the skills of The PGPG. Choose your preferred method of travel, and realize that while you are not in your hometown, you are still the perfect gentleman. When traveling the perfect gentleman knows:

- Have a valid passport ready and available at all times. It takes a few moments every decade, so there is no excuse not to have one readily available. Besides, you want to get those stamps, which are a nice badge when you travel.

- Always be equipped with the things you need for the trip, including mobile device, computer, swimsuit, fresh clothing and so forth. You never know who you could meet to open new opportunities.

- Do some research on the country or city you are going to before you arrive. You can even do it on your way there with the power of the internet and mobile devices. It is good to know a few current events so that you are abreast during small conversations with locals.

- Know key words, phrases, how to greet different ladies and gents and how to tip at meals. Things may be a bit different than what you are accustomed to. Adapt and adjust accordingly, even if the locals look at you like you're from another planet.

- If you're on a leisure trip, remember to relax and enjoy life. That is why we are on earth in the first place. Do not get caught up in constantly checking emails and other business activities.

- If there are any emergencies that may happen when away, there should be a few people who know how to reach you wherever you are, at all times. Inform those people before you leave.

Ferrera Fresh Tip: Always do a little research about the country you are visiting or have your assistant or someone else do it for you.

Below you will find a list of the most popular languages spoken around the world from the countries visited the most, at the time of this printing. These simple words can possibly get you through the day should there be an emergency. Try them, study them, reference them and use them as you *need*.

Most Popular Languages Spoken Around The World

English	Spanish	French	Italian	Portuguese	German
Hello	Hola	Bonjour	Ciao	Olá	Hallo
Thank you	Gracias	Merci	Grazie	Obrigado	Vielen Dank
Yes	Si	Oui	Si	Sim	Ja
No	No	Non	No	Não	Keine
Restroom	Baño	Toilettes	Restroom	Banheiro	Toilette
Food	Comida	Nourriture	Cibo	Alimentos	Labensmittel
Airport	Aeropuerto	Aéroport	Aeroporto	Aeroporto	Flughafen
Help	Ayuda	Aider	Aiuto	Ajuda	Hilfe
Good Bye	Adiós	Au revoir	Arrivederci	Adeus	Auf Wiedersehen

The Perfect Gentleman is the Perfect Guest

If you are ever a guest in someone's home, treat it *better* than your own. Be cautious not to break or destroy anything, minimize bathroom time and respect the bedtime of others. Above all, remember they are welcoming you in and appreciate it. As a guest the perfect gentleman knows:

◆ Do not over stay your welcome. It is important that you know how long you plan to stay as does your host. If plans change, inform your host immediately, not at the last minute.

- Thank your host three times for your stay. As you arrive verbally, as you leave verbally and when you get home by mailing a thank you card or small gift. Yes, you can bring or leave a parting gift if you have planned ahead.

- Even if you do not make your bed at home, you *should* do it as a guest. The only exceptions are if there is a cleaning service or if the person has asked you not to. Try making the bed soon after you arise.

- Eat, sleep, and play according to their rules. If there are things you must do, or do not agree with, respectfully share it with your host.

- If you forget something small like toothpaste or a towel, simply ask. Most people understand since they have already let you into their home.

Ferrera Fresh Tip: Remain humble and respectful in any situation, which will eventually become natural for the perfect gentleman.

Wine Tasting

A wine tasting is a nice event to attend to mix and mingle with ladies and other gentlemen. It is designed for you to taste a variety of different wines in one session; it is not designed for you to get drunk. If you're a wine drinker or want to experience wine, attend a wine event with good company. Whether you're attending your first wine tasting event of you're a regular, there's a few things to remember:

- You do not have to drink or taste every wine. Choose those that interest you and opt for a small taste.

- A drink is when you swallow the wine after tasting it in your mouth. A taste is when the wine goes into your mouth and you spit it out into the appropriate bucket after you get the taste. Yes, it is okay to spit.

- Remember to keep your same glass throughout the event unless otherwise stated by the host. You can rinse the glass with water that should be provided.

- When you have a glass of wine, give it a little swirl so the beautiful aroma can hit the air. Not too hard of a swirl to spill, but be confident in your swirling technique. Give the wine a whiff to smell it and then taste, taking a sip and letting it roll around in your mouth.

- You can occasionally have a second taste or pour the remaining wine gently into the waste bucket, which should be on or near the table. Then move on to the next wine.

Ferrera Fresh Tip: Practice swirling and drinking with your left hand to leave your right hand free to shake hands while you mix and mingle with others.

How to Spit Wine

- It is okay to spit out the wine at a tasting event; it is not rude. In fact, it can be viewed as respectable at times because it shows that you know what you are doing.

- When spitting wine, form your mouth as if you are whistling and blow the wine out of your mouth into the designated bin. This gives an even, controlled spit, minimizing any mess.

- If you do make a small mess, don't worry about it. This is understood at wine events. Just do not let it happen too often. Remember to keep your handkerchief handy for quick wipes of your mouth.

Ferrera Fresh Tip: You do not spit wine out at the dinner table, only at events where spitting is allowed.

Ordering Wine

Ordering wine from the vast lists we now see can be just as challenging as choosing who you may want to share it with. If you choose to drink wine, you will find some varieties that you like and others you do not like. Take mental notes and order accordingly. Remember, wine does not have to be expensive to be good. A great idea when in doubt is to ask your server what he or she recommends and why. If you like their response, then proceed by ordering. When it comes to ordering wine the perfect gentleman knows:

- Ask your guests if they care for a glass and if they have a wine preference.

- You do not *need* to know all the fancy wine names, but it is quite cool if you do know how to pronounce them. One way to get around saying awkward names is to ask the server "How do I pronounce this wine?" (while you point at it). Then repeat it back the same way it was pronounced. It may get a cute chuckle out of the lady you are with as well.

- Take a mental note of what you like for ordering in the future. Needless to say, take note of price as well to order with more ease.

- Know a little bit about *types* of wine prior to ordering. There are basically two types: red or white.

- White wines are great with chicken, fish, pasta, rice and many times, light colored food. Just as red wines are great with steak, lamb, other red meats, vegetables, bread or cheese.

- It is okay to hold a glass of red wine by the bowl because you can drink red wine at room temperature. With a glass of white wine hold it by the stem to keep the wine from getting too warm from the temperature of your hand.

- Remember, there are no "have to dos" when pairing a wine with your meal. If you enjoy a particular white wine and you're having a steak or any other combination, by all means do it. There are no rules to enjoyment.

> *Ferrera Fresh Tip*: Research the wine list, if available, prior to arriving to enhance your knowledge.

The Perfect Gentleman's Quick Reference on Wine

Types of Red Wine	Tastes Like	Looks Like	Pairs Well With
Barbera (Bar-BEHR-uh)	Often Spritzy & Fruity	Deep Ruby color	Blend with other reds, Bold flavor cheese
Cabernet Sauvignon (Cab-er-NAY SO-vin-yon)	Plum, Blackberry, Blueberry, Vanilla	Dark Purple or Ruby	Red Meat, Red Pasta, Lamb or Chocolate
Merlot (Mur-LO)	Cherries, Plums Blackberries & Chocolate	Dark Reddish Purple	Poultry, Pork, Red Meat, Pastas
Pinot Noir (Pee-NO NWA)	Sweet red berries, plums, cherry tomatoes	Reddish Burgundy	Poultry, Beef, Fish or Pork
Shiraz (Shih-RAHZ)	Roasted sweet peppers, black cherry & licorice	Deep Purple Color	Grilled Meat & Veggies, Red Meat or Pizza

The Perfect Gentleman's Quick Reference on Wine

Types of White Wine	Tastes Like	Looks Like	Pairs Well With
Chardonnay (Shar-dun-NAY)	Like tart white grapes & pears	A light gold color	Nuts, cheese, pasta Very versatile
Pinot Grigio (Pee-No-GREE-zho)	Similar to Chardonnay with a Sweeter twist	A clear Yellowish color	White cheeses and cream based pasta
Sauvignon Blanc (SO-vin-yon BLAHNK)	A mixture of several fruits	Crisp bold yellow or Gold color	Cheese and red tomato pasta dishes
Riesling (Rees-Ling)	Often very sweet & crisp	Light almost tan or Beige color	Caviar, smoked salmon and Game poultry
Viognier (Vee-oh-YAY)	Sweet Apricots & Peach	Pale yellow or Honey color	Scallops, shrimp or Salty fish dishes

Cigarettes, Cigars and Other Smokes

Tobacco cigars are one of the original forms of smokes consumed by man. Cigarettes became more popular after the French began to consume a smaller form more regularly. Thus "small cigar" or cigar *plus* ette equals cigarette. When smoking, the perfect gentleman knows:

♦ Any cigar or cigarette should be consumed only by those of proper age with no exception.

♦ The occasional cigar can be enjoyable for celebratory purposes such as winning a championship, a wedding celebration with the groom or other event you deem worthy of celebrating, like the birth of a newborn (not around the newborn, of course).

♦ At some establishments they may offer a cigar after the meal. Partake in one if you would like, but it is okay to pass when it is offered. This is not perceived as being disrespectful. It is also okay to take one to go if it is allowed.

♦ If you are in groups of other nonsmokers consider turning your head *up*, blowing your smoke *up* in the air rather than forward where more people can be exposed directly to the smoke.

♦ If someone asks you not to smoke around them, do not get angry. Simply change location or stop for the moment as requested.

♦ When offering cigars to others, extend the cigar case to the person and let them take a cigar for themselves. It is also better to let the person light their own cigar, so they have more control.

- Always dispose of cigarette butts properly in ashtrays. If ashtrays are not present that is a sign that smoking may not be allowed in that particular area.

- Always allow cigar butts to burn away slowly in the ashtray. Do not mash it out to get rid of the light. Doing so will cause an unpleasant scent.

- At times cigarettes and other smokes can lead to other illegal drugs and a gentleman NEVER indulges in any type of drugs, no matter how harmful or not harmful. If it does occur, and it becomes a problem, get help, forgive yourself, and carry on with life. Call 800.729.6687 or visit www.ncadi.samhsa.gov for drug and alcohol information.

> *Ferrera Fresh Tip*: As we all know, smoking does cause cancer. Remember that your body is your only temple and if you treat it well, it will treat you well.

Surprise Parties

Throw them only for people who will enjoy them. If someone throws one for you, and it's not exactly a "surprise," act surprised. It is okay to tell them you knew at a later point. If you find out prior to the party and you rather not have it, calmly let the person know by thanking them first and suggesting a different option.

> *Ferrera Fresh Tip*: Try not to be the last person to leave a party unless it's for a pleasant lady and she is aware that you are waiting for her.

BYOB or BYOF

Bring Your Own Booze or Food is not the event of choice for a gentleman. Be selective in attending them often and only host these types of events with a *few* very close friends. As the perfect gentleman, when you invite people to your location, *host* them. Yes, it can get costly, but you can plan and maybe collaborate with a few people to minimize costs. Try not to require people to bring their own booze or bring their own food.

Splitting the Bill

Splitting the bill among groups has become more popular now and is not the easiest task to do. However, some people do host these types of gatherings and you must be a gentleman. Do your best to always have cash to simplify your portion of the bill and be open to giving more than what your portion of the meal costs. Eliminate any arguments and "I paid, you paid, I don't want to pay gratuity" conversations. Know the people you are attending with and choose to attend selectively. Remember, as the perfect gentleman, minimize hosting these sorts of events. Only host them with a handful of close friends, occasionally.

Leaving an Event

When to leave an event is completely up to you. However, when leaving an event at least say good-bye to the host and thank them for the invite. The same applies with a simple wave or a tip of the hat to the bar or club owner, if you know who he or she is. Do your best to wave, wink, hug, and shake hands with those you know while heading toward the exit. There's no need for long explanations as to why you're leaving. Give your reason and move on. If you're simply ready to go, at least inform the host. If a crowd is not to your liking, try to embrace it for a bit and then gracefully leave.

The Perfect Gentleman Plays a Joke

Playing pranks, laughing and cracking jokes with others can be fun and can even build on a relationship if the person eventually laughs with you. Please, please, please be cautious of the type of joke and who is on the receiving end. The best thing to do is consider the person's possible reaction and their personality. If you know them well, *hopefully* that helps. In any situation, within a short time make sure it's known that it is a joke and remember the perfect gentleman never makes offensive jokes about a person's race, religion, gender, or sexual orientation.

As the perfect gentleman, it is important to know that there is a time to have fun and a time to be serious. Even as a mature adult, it is nice to enjoy a variety of social environments with ladies and gentleman alike. The key to making leisure events the most enjoyable is to display your characteristics as the perfect gentleman. Be considerate of others. Be timely, cordial and respectful by interacting with the other guests around you.

Yes, the perfect gentleman handles business, but he has a handle on social interaction as well. In social environments, remember that your presence will attract other respectful gentlemen and, of course, ladies. Enjoy!

7

The Perfect Gentleman

Dines In and Dines Out with Manners

When dining in, it is easy to become lackadaisical with the proper eating etiquette, and contrary to popular belief at times you can! However, this does not mean that you do not know the right way to eat. At times we all want to have a soda or a beer and eat our food on the couch with fingers messy because of the hot wings and French fries while watching a football game on TV. The few times that you can do this are when you are eating alone in private, when your wife is out of town or when you are not expecting any guests. If that is not the case, full table manners and eating etiquette apply. Practice your eating and table manners regularly and know *when* to use them, which is every time you are around others.

Ferrera Fresh Tip: Dining with the perfect gentleman should be an enjoyable experience, even if the food itself is not so enjoyable.

Dining Out

Dining out is an experience that the perfect gentleman truly enjoys with good company. On the contrary, eating out can be very uneventful when with the wrong people. Please know that as the perfect gentleman, you are never the wrong person.

Even if you are dining out by yourself, I recommend you always behave as if someone is watching you, because someone might be. If they are not, then at least you're always on point.

Using Your Napkin

When dining at a place where there is a fabric napkin, it will be placed to the *left* of your plate or between your knife and fork, which is how you determine where to sit. When using the napkin while dining the perfect gentleman knows:

♦ Your napkin should be placed on your lap before you begin eating and should never be tucked in the collar of your shirt.

♦ Your napkin should not be shaken open when removing it from the table. Your napkin should be taken from the table and unfolded out of sight on your lap.

- If the napkin is wrapped around the utensils, the same applies. Calmly *unwrap* the utensils without making distracting clanging noise on the table.

- When using your napkin, blot or dab your mouth with an edge of the napkin rather than wipe as you would with a washcloth.

- If you leave the table during a meal, place the napkin to the side of your plate or on the seat, with fork and knife in the correct position on your plate.

- When finished with your meal, do not ball up your napkin or place it on your plate. You should set it loosely on the table in front of you.

Using Utensils

The perfect gentleman always knows which utensil to use and when to use it. Your forks are on the left side of your plate, or napkin that is in the center. Your knife is on the right side. Learn this and remember it as it applies to any dining table. Using your utensils starting with the one farthest from your plate is standard procedure. Then work your way in toward the plate for each course. When using your utensils the perfect gentleman knows:

- While you are eating, no one needs to hear your fork, knife or any other utensil consistently clinking and hitting your plate.

- Use the fork and knife in the proper hands at all times. The knife should always be in your dominant hand and your fork in the other.

- Do not tuck your tie in your shirt or swing it over your shoulder while eating. That just does not look cool! Practice eating properly and you will not have to worry about mess.

- When dining at Asian restaurants only use chopsticks if you know how to use them properly, never for jokes or to make fun. Learn how to use them in a private setting or when out with someone who can teach you the proper way.

- When eating international cuisines that require eating with your hands, remember to wash your hands before eating and only touch food you plan to eat.

> *Ferrera Fresh Tip:* Practice eating correctly as much as possible. With a little practice, you'll be eating like a prestigious king.

Dining with Others

- If there are place tags at the meal you are attending, always sit where your name card is and do not change it.

- If someone takes your items, like a fork by accident, ask your server to bring you a new one. Do not ask anyone to give you their fork or point out someone's mistake in public. Just politely ask the waiter for another.

- Passing a fork when someone takes yours might only be acceptable in private family settings. In that case, make sure you teach that person what is correct for their future knowledge.

- If you are setting a table for guests, try to place every setting with the same style utensils, plates and cups. Never set a table with any glass or plate that has any chips or cracks.

- When sitting at a table, take a glance and sit in a way that alternate the seats for male and female, which allows for a husband and wife to sit next to each other.

- In singles environments, alternating seats by male and female can encourage interaction. Just never sit people next to others who may cause them to be uncomfortable.

- If hosting a meal at a rectangular table, the gentleman should sit at the head of the table and his wife to the right.

- Men should sit at the head of the table and at seats closest to the nearest exit, offering a sign of protection from anyone unexpectedly entering the room.

- If someone asks you to pass only the salt or only the pepper, pass *both* the salt and pepper. The salt and pepper should always be together so that the next person who asks for either does not have to look around the table for one or the other. If you ask, remember to always ask for both the salt and pepper.

- Taste your food at least once before adding any salt or pepper to it. It can sometimes be disrespectful to the chef.

- When an item is passed like a breadbasket from the center of the table, offer it to the person directly to your right first. Then take your portion and pass the dish around the table to your left.

- Begin eating only after the last person at your table has received their plate.

- If another gentleman suggests that you begin eating, but his food has not yet arrived and there are no ladies present, you may choose to eat or wait for his food to arrive. If there are women present, or if a lady offers, it is best to wait for her food to arrive.

- Be sure to keep your elbows and arms close to your side while eating in order to not disturb others next to you.

- If someone prays or says grace based on religious beliefs you do not agree with, just simply remain quiet. If you choose to pray, you can invite others to pray with you as well, even in public.

- When dining with children make sure to help them and be cautious not to allow them to disturb neighboring guests. Note that some fine dining establishments do not allow children.

- Allow ladies and children to order their food first. Fine dining restaurants will know this. However, if your server does not know and asks you to order first, kindly offer the lady to order by saying her name with a slight nod of your head, letting her order.

- When ordering your food, remember to include all special requests at the time you order. If you forget a special request, ask your waiter if the chef has started preparing your food. If your meal preparation has not started, make your special request. If the meal is already being prepared, consider accepting it as it is unless you are allergic to something.

- If any silverware drops on the floor, do not pick it up and put it back on the table. Slide it close to the table with your foot so it is out of the way, but let someone hosting pick it up and ask for new utensils. Napkins, however, can be picked up if dropped.

- Use common sense. If something drops in a walking area, simply pick it up and hold for a short period until you can hand it to someone who can take care of it.

Buffet

- When eating at a buffet the same dining etiquette applies. Women and children first and begin eating once everyone has arrived back to the table.

- Be patient in buffet lines. There's no need to make frustrating sounds or pout because the line is taking too long. Just chat with a friend while you wait.

- Do not pile your plate with a mountain of food. There is enough and you can go back as often as you want. If something does run out, just visit that establishment at another time.

- Whenever you go back for another serving or one small item get a new clean plate. Do not take a plate that you have already eaten from back to the buffet court. Too many germs can be passed if you do this.

- If someone asks you to get something for them as you head to the buffet court, bring it to them on a new separate plate. Do not put it on your plate for them to take.

Ferrera Fresh Tip: Be the perfect gentleman at the buffet court. Eat properly as you normally would in any dining setting.

DURING THE MEAL

Salad

◆ Salad can sometimes be eaten without a knife, with the fork in your dominant hand. Some salads do require a little cutting with a knife and the same applies with the knife in the dominant hand and the fork in the other.

Bread

◆ When eating any bread (bread sticks, dinner rolls, etc.), remember to minimize what you touch when selecting your portion if the bread is taken from a basket.

◆ If you choose to put butter on your bread, do not butter the whole bread all at once. Break the bread into the portion you are going to eat at that moment and butter that piece. This will allow you to eat your bread neater.

◆ At breakfast meals you can butter your whole slice of toast, pancakes or waffles on your plate.

> *Ferrera Fresh Tip*: Do not use your bread as a utensil to slide food onto your fork. A light dipping of bread sticks into sauce is fine, but use a fork and knife to take up your food.

Appetizers

◆ Appetizers are usually meant to be shared and enjoyed together. Although you may be hungry, be mindful of others when taking your portion.

◆ The perfect gentleman kindly offers others to indulge when the appetizers arrive.

- Do not double dip anything. It might be so tempting, but refrain from doing it. If you feel like you will need more dip, consider putting some on your plate and eat to your liking. This also applies to finger foods at parties.

Main Entrée

- Often times the main entrée is composed of steak, chicken or fish, among other options. When eating these items start with the prongs of your fork facedown into the item, holding it in steady.

- Then with the knife in your other hand, cut near the fork for a desired piece. As you eat the piece the fork now holds, the fork can remain in the same direction as you place it in your mouth.

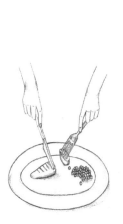

Dessert

♦ The purpose of dessert was originally so that the sugar would keep you awake after your meal, but that is not always the case. With that in mind, choose your desserts and proportions of desserts accordingly.

♦ When dessert arrives, it is just another part of the meal, so all eating etiquette applies.

♦ The spoon at the top of your plate is for coffee or tea after the meal. The fork above your plate is for your dessert.

♦ If a spoon is needed for your dessert, it should be brought with the dessert. If not, ask for one.

♦ If you happen to be sharing a dessert, know that all food sharing etiquette guidelines apply. Allow ladies and children to indulge first, and only touch and take portions you are going to eat.

Beverages

♦ When eating at dinner the perfect gentleman knows that the drink glasses are placed near the top right side of your plate and the bread plate is near the top slightly to the left. There is no need to ask the person next to you.

♦ If someone uses your glass by accident, ask the server for a new glass.

♦ If there is a wine glass and you choose not to have wine, do not turn the glass upside down. Simply notify the server when he or she comes that you will not be having wine. The same rule applies for coffee cups and anything else.

- Remember, you do not always have to take the refill when it is offered.

- Even if you are really thirsty, always drink smoothly. Do not gulp.

> *Ferrera Fresh Tip*: When drinking any beverage, as a gentleman, there is no need to have your pinky in the air. This is sometimes done by women, even though neither should do it.

Coffee

- Coffee or tea often is served after dinner since the caffeine is designed to keep you awake.

- Be considerate and make sure there is enough cream and sugar to go around. If it runs out, ask for more.

- If the sugar is served in the form of cubes, use the tongs that are designed for them, not your fingers. If it is not there, ask your server for it or use a clean spoon to grab your desired cubes.

- If the sugar is in packages, fold the packets and place them under the rim of cup saucer or bread plate.

- After using your stirring spoon, do not lick it or put it in your mouth. Just rest in on your saucer or on a napkin.

- If your sugar is in a cup to be scooped, remember to use the spoon that is designed for the sugar. If there is none, use your spoon and put your sugar in your coffee first, then your cream, so that you do not put a used spoon back into the sugar cup.

- If you do not want coffee or tea after your meal, just indicate to the server when you are asked. You do not need to turn your cup upside down.

UNDERSTANDING UNFAMILIAR OR AWKWARD ITEMS

Soup

*   Soup is a very enjoyable, simple dish, but it is often spilled because of not being eaten correctly. Remember, your soup spoon is the larger round spoon that is brought with your soup. It is not often set on the table.

*   When eating soup, rather than moving the spoon in a direction toward your body, spoon away from your body and then lift up holding the spoon even. Now bring the spoon to your mouth to enjoy without spilling. You may lean over a bit so as not to spill and continue the same process as you neatly enjoy your soup.

*   If you choose to blow your soup to cool it, remember to do so in a light and gentle manner.

*   If you are able to, try to put the whole spoon into your mouth to avoid slurping. Do not slurp your soup; you're the perfect gentleman.

Round Tomatoes

◆ Try to eat the whole small tomato at once to avoid squirting juice or having it roll all around your plate. If you are unable to, place the knife touching the tomato like a wall and poke the tomato with your fork to hold it in place. Then cut the tomato in half with the knife in a gentle sawing motion to avoid squirting and eat each portion individually.

Olives

◆ Similar to those little round tomatoes, try to eat the whole olive at once. If not, cut them as you would round tomatoes.

Lemon and Lime

◆ If you choose to squeeze lemon, lime, or orange wedge into your beverage, cover your cup with one hand, (creating a cone-shaped lid) and with the other hand squeeze the lemon into your beverage under your covering hand. That way, if any juice from the lemon misses the cup, it will be protected by your covering hand, not disturbing anyone else around. The same etiquette applies when squeezing lemon juice on fish or seafood or anything else you choose.

Crab Legs, Lobster and Shellfish

◆ Lobster and crab legs are to be held in one hand and a shellfish cracker in the other hand.

◆ Remove meat with a shellfish fork or spatula, which is the tiny fork that is brought with your shellfish.

- If eating any of these hot, consider dipping them in melted butter or tartar sauce.

- If eating any of these cold, consider dipping them in mayonnaise, tartar sauce, or other special sauces.

- Use a large bowl or platter to discard shells. Most of the time this will be provided for you at the restaurant.

- The finger bowls with warm water and lemons are for you to lightly clean your fingers when you are finished, not to wash your hands.

Escargot

- Escargot or gourmet snails are a dish often served as an appetizer. If you like them, please enjoy. If you have never had them, do not let what it is stop you from trying.

- Escargot should be eaten with a fork, not your hands. Similar to crab legs or shellfish, grab the edible meat part from out of the shell, chew and swallow. You do not need to crack the shell when eating escargot.

"What Am I Eating"

- When you do not know what the food is that is in front of you, it is okay to ask. It is best to ask the person who has served it. If they do not know, ask someone next to you that may know or who has the same thing.

- As you ask, do not frown or make faces in disgust. Kindly ask and move on. The perfect gentleman does not need to offend anyone.

"I Don't Like This"

◆ If you eat something you immediately do not like, remain calm. Panicking can cause you to act irrationally.

◆ Do not spit it out, run away or cough rudely. It is best to put the fork back to your mouth and take it out and put it on the side of your plate.

◆ It is also okay to use two fingers and discretely remove the item from your mouth and place it to the side of your plate, under bread or garnish.

◆ America has made it common to spit your food in a napkin if you do not like something. However, this only makes sense if you are using a disposable napkin that you will not use again.

◆ The most important thing to remember is to be polite. If you do not like something you eat, be considerate of those around you.

BEING APPROPRIATE IN AWKWARD DINING MOMENTS

Choking

If you are chocking and drinking water does not help, excuse yourself from the table with a hand signal to someone you are dining with so they are aware of your situation. If another person looks like they are choking, monitor the situation, but let them care for themselves initially. Assist them when they motion for help or if it looks severe. Do not panic, but keep your cell phone handy.

Something in Your Teeth

If there is something between your teeth and simple tongue movements do not help remove it, do not put your finger in your mouth at the table. Doing this at the table is inappropriate and completely disgusting. Using a toothpick, business card or anything else is inappropriate as well. Simply excuse yourself to the restroom and take care of it.

Something Spills

If something spills at the table, do not get embarrassed for yourself or anyone else. A gentleman always keeps his cool, even when a mistake is made. First, try to stop the spill from spreading. Second, clean it as soon as possible or inform the host. Finally, move on! We all make mistakes. If it is you who spills, pull yourself together quickly and help a bit with the clean up. Never rudely joke if it is someone else's mistake. If someone spills on their clothes and it looks like they have tried to clean it, do not bring the embarrassing moment back to light.

A Crying Baby

If a child is crying, try to calm them first. If the crying persists, simply leave the table. If it is someone else's child, please do not make faces in annoyance. The parent may already be uncomfortable.

Sharing Food

If you share food with someone else while eating, let them take the food from your plate. If you are eating with a lady and she does not mind you feeding her a taste of your food, you can. Select small portions to share and avoid spilling. Put the fork or spoon close enough to her mouth so that she can bring her mouth to it and eat. When taking your fork or spoon back, gently slide your whole arm back toward yourself, keeping the fork or spoon even. A little practice and you'll have ladies eating out of your hand in more than one way.

Lack of Conversation

As the perfect gentleman, a lack of conversation should never happen. See Chapter 4.

Finishing a Meal

♦ Do not stack plates in an attempt to make it easier for the waiter. This can be viewed as a sign of being impatience to the waiter.

♦ Do not hail your waiter by raising your hand and pointing at your plate. The server will eventually come. If they do not, grab their attention by making eye contact and nodding for them to come over. This also applies while you are eating your meal and you need something.

"I'm still eating."

♦ Do not push your plate away. When you are finished eating, place your napkin to the left of your plate with the used area not showing.

"I'm done eating."

184

Paying for the Meal

- The person who invites you to the meal is usually the one who pays. But as the perfect gentleman always be prepared to pay.

- Treat ladies as well as elders to their meal as much as possible. It is also not a problem for a gentleman to treat other gents to a meal. If you are the recipient of the complimentary meal, respectfully return the favor on another occasion.

- It is okay to occasionally "go Dutch," where each person pays for his or her own meal. Just make sure it is understood prior to eating.

- To avoid the awkward "who pays" moment, contact the restaurant maitre d' of an establishment before you arrive to give them your paying information. Ask them to add a minimum of 18% gratuity and never bring the bill to the table. This avoids the awkward, "who pays" moment and your guest may be impressed.

- Paying for the meal does not always include paying for spirits or any open bar tabs prior to the meal. However, drinks ordered during the meal are part of the meal, so just be mindful or make arrangements with those drinking.

- Tipping for service is a must and is given relative to the quality of service received. Unless the service is completely unacceptable, some monetary tip should be given, even if the service is poor.

- Not-so-good service can equate to a not-so-good tip and vice versa. Good service deserves a good tip.

Ferrera Fresh Tip: The maitre d' is French for "master waiter," which is the person responsible for assigning customer tables. If you can build relationships with a few good ones, you're in luck.

Leaving a Meal

- Remember to thank the establishment for service rendered, even if it is a simple verbal "thank you" on the way out the door.

- If the service is well above expectations, it is appropriate to personally thank the manager or maitre d', if available.

- If service is below your expectations, it is okay to make mention to the manager, not your server or anyone else.

- When you give a complaint to a restaurant you do not need to be rude when offering a suggestion. It will even make your complaint more valid when you are polite.

- Remember that the purpose of a complaint is not to receive anything in return but to improve future service for yourself and others. You can choose whether you go to the establishment again or not.

- Of course, open and hold doors for ladies and others as you exit.

Ferrera Fresh Tip: Treating others to a meal is a nice gesture and the perfect gentleman knows it is more of a blessing to give than to receive.

Dining in or dining out should be an enjoyable experience with the perfect gentleman. Yes, mishaps may occur, but you still can display grace and class in any situation. By being respectful to others around you and understanding you are there for food and fellowship will allow you to be at your best. So, have fun dining. Embrace good company. Enjoy your meal.

8
The Perfect Gentleman
With the Ladies

Believe it or not, every social interaction we have with the ladies counts for something. Women are likely to remember far more than men do in most social interactions. In this chapter, it is important to use the things that work for you and ditch the things that do not. You will, in time, if you haven't already, find the characteristics that make you unique among the ladies. If there are only a few things you remember from this section, remember to always be confident, be yourself and be respectful. These three things alone will allow you to at least start with the upper hand when interacting with ladies. With that said, let's embark upon the perfect gentleman with the ladies.

Ferrera Fresh Tip: Ladies are naturally attracted to a confident gentleman. Make sure to always display confidence, and you might even have her at hello.

First Things First

As the perfect gentleman, you will naturally find yourself among ladies—plural. This does not mean dating or being in relationships with multiple ladies. It means, as a gentleman, ladies will be attracted to you simply for good company and, of course, for more intimate relationships. Ladies can be elders, relatives, coworkers, business professionals, platonic friends and so on. All ladies will be attracted to your grace as a gentleman, not always for a personal relationship. Ladies love to be in the presence of a graceful, respectful and confident man.

Young or old, women are one of the most precious gifts our Creator has placed on this earth and we as gentlemen should appreciate, respect and cherish a lady at all times. Yes, I know ladies are not always so perfect, just like us, but still, we should appreciate and embrace their greatness. Finally, as ladies become attracted to you, it is your job to humbly accept the fact that women will naturally be attracted to you as the perfect gentleman. It is important to control your confidence while embracing their presence as well.

Approaching a Lady

As you have heard before, "You never get a second chance to make a first impression." It is true. When approaching a lady for the first time, just to say "hello." Ditch the so-called cool pick-up lines or catch phrases. Most of them are overrated and are too childish for her to take you seriously. As the perfect gentleman, you don't need to do the things every other guy does to get her interested. Just being a sincere person will allow a conversation to be started. Remember, all ladies will not be interested in you for the purpose of dating, but all ladies will be interested in a gentleman for the sake of good company, and there is nothing wrong with that. It might, in fact, be to your advantage. As the perfect gentleman, when approaching ladies you are interested in remember:

◆ She is still a person and should receive the same respect as anyone else you meet or interact with.

◆ In the past, there was a time when a man should not shake hands with a woman. This no longer applies and it is perfectly fine to shake hands with her when you first meet.

◆ Shake hands as you normally would while being a bit gentler. If there is anything more such as a social kiss or hug, be selective on when to initiate it.

◆ When meeting a lady in a social setting a simple nod of the head is enough and can be just as friendly as a handshake.

◆ Approach her when you are facing each other and have made eye contact. Do not sneak up on her from behind.

◆ Listening and eye contact are of huge importance. It shows you are interested, paying attention and focused.

◆ Keep introduction conversations short and sweet. Sometimes thirty seconds to two minutes is enough time for the perfect gentleman to leave a positive impression.

- You also may not want to ask for contact information right away. Try to connect with her once again before your leave the environment, and then proceed to ask for information as you wish.

- Try to introduce yourself first and let her finish your sentence by telling you her name. For example, "Good day. My name is Michael Ferrera and your name is…" This allows her the opportunity to talk and start the conversation if she wants to.

- The perfect gentleman is never bothered if turned down by a lady. Always approach her with the intention of saying hello and converse with her normally.

> *Ferrera Fresh Tip*: Never be intimidated to approach any lady. Remain confident and humble in knowing that your approach may turn out to be just a general hello.

Awkward Encounters

What if you see a lady of interest at an airport, library, or in a public place where you might not ever see her again? Well, you have to make your move. Still approach her just to say *hello* as you normally would. Be confident and be yourself. A few things to consider in this situation as the perfect gentleman are:

- She may be interested and she may not. Listen, learn, take mental notes and move on accordingly. She may be sincerely busy and not have time to talk, so you must be ready to accept that, period.

- A sincere introductory comment might be, "I apologize for interrupting you, but I noticed you from afar and I wanted to at least say hello. My name is. . .and yours is. . ." (let her talk). Repeat her name in a slow, joyous sound so you remember it and begin a brief conversation.

- Do not be upset or sad if she is not interested. You can ask if you can talk at a later date by exchanging contacts. Again, she may not be in the right mindset at that time to be approached by a man that is interested.

Ferrera Fresh Tip: Remember every female you approach may not be fit for you as a gentleman. Be respectful and accept that you do not need to talk to every lady or ask for every number.

After a Connection

The second interaction, or your first interaction after a contact is made, should be with a phone call. A phone call is much more personal than leaving text messages, social media messages and the other forms of communication. If there is no answer when you first call, that is fine. This might be to your advantage because it is in her control to get back to you. Leave a short pleasant message and ask her to call you back. For example, "Hello <u>Her Name</u>. It was a pleasure to meet you on <u>insert</u>

Ferrera Fresh Tip: After your charm with the ladies has become commonplace is when you are at your best as the perfect gentleman.

<u>date or location</u>. You may remember our conversation about <u>insert topic accordingly</u>. When you have a moment, you are welcome to call me at <u>Your Phone Number</u>. I look forward to talking with you. " Then end with your favorite salutation.

No Return Call

If she does not call back, it is okay. Wait a while. Four days to a week is best. It might be best to call again rather than send a text message. She may want to see if you will give up quick. If the same response happens, a short text may work to get attention. If not, be wise and determine if it is time to move on.

When to Move On

There is no exact answer as to *when* to move on, but just be wise. Be a gentleman. I have found that if you attempt contact four or more times with no communication in return, you may want to rethink her interest in you. This is only the case for new ladies you meet. If a relationship has already been established, that is a different situation, which we will address later.

Setting Up the Date

Ladies have busy lives as well and you do not want to be left with the statement, "I already have plans." Text message date arrangements are best when you are already dating or if that is what *she* prefers. Pick up the phone to call her, have a conversation and plan the date. When setting a date, don't beat around the bush. Ask general and simple questions to find out what her calendar is like and set up a date with her by simply asking. Many guys miss opportunities simply because they don't ask. Do not let that be you.

Ferrera Fresh Tip: You do not have to actually use the word "date" when asking her out. Women use that word. Just ask her out.

The First Date

The first date is the most important date, period! It is your opportunity to display the perfect gentleman that you are and to observe and learn about the lady you are interested in. Listening and good conversation will make this date successful. Be confident and humble as the perfect gentleman and remember that the tips in this book can assist you before, during or after the first date. On first dates the perfect gentleman knows:

◆ Make sure to plan this date. It shows her that you take time and that she is important. There is no excuse not to plan the first date.

◆ Know a little about the weather for the day or night and a little bit about the things she likes or does not like as it pertains to food, fun and entertainment.

◆ There is no need for too much touching or being close on a first date. If it does happen, let her initiate it. She may *continually* and subtly invite you to be closer to her with small touches, and other signs of flirting. Just take notes, keep your cool and respond accordingly.

◆ The first date should be a place where you can actually talk. Movies, operas or plays just do not work since you have to be silent in these places. Having dinner, a glass of wine, a cup of coffee or a lounge is more appropriate since you can interact in conversation.

◆ Be creative on your first date. However, when in doubt, or if you just want to keep it simple, a dinner date always works.

- Be very alert on the first date. Listen, respond, remember, take metal notes and know that all communication skills apply. Her body language and conversation will tell you whether this is the only date or if there will be dates to follow.

- Dress your best at all times. You already know this, but put your skills into play from Chapter 3.

- Holding hands, kissing and other romantic gestures on a first date are not *necessary*. It might be in your best interest not to do these things anyway. Think about it; you are examining her just as she is examining you.

- By keeping your composure and not being too romantic on a first date might make her want you even more. As the perfect gentleman, it will give the impression that you are polite enough to respect her space and she will be attracted to that.

- Be on time. She may make you wait just a bit for no *real* reason, but that's fine. It's probably worth it. Mobile devices can keep you occupied while waiting, but the moment she's ready, all attention should be on her.

> *Ferrera Fresh Tip*: Be creative on your first date. A movie should not be an option. You cannot really converse and get to know each other in a movie theatre.

The Second Date

The second date is almost as important as the first. However, you have proven yourself to be a gentleman from your first date. Movie theatres and places where talking is not conducive are still not options since you still want to get to know her more. Hopefully you've had a good phone conversation or two between dates that have allowed you to learn a little more about her. Remember that on the second date you are both still gathering information about each other, so observe and know that you are being observed. On the second date the perfect gentleman knows:

◆ You are still in full "impress" mode. Not until you are fully dating and you are both comfortable can you show up in flip-flops and a T-shirt on casual dates. So, dress up and be at your best.

◆ Begin to talk about more than just surface information like jobs and where she's from. Talk about things like why she's interested. What brought her back on another date? Learning this will help you know what she likes and what you need to keep doing if you want her around.

◆ A second date is when she *might* share a little more of herself with you. One of the most important things on this date is to take good mental note and listen, listen, listen.

◆ Keep your cool, show your swagger and your personality as the perfect gentleman. A second date opportunity will eventually become the norm for you as the perfect gentleman.

♦ In regards to kissing, hugging, and closeness on the second date, use just as much discretion as the first date. Be cautious, but feel free to partake if you wish and more importantly if she lets you. Let her *feel* like she is always in control, even when you are.

> *Ferrera Fresh Tip:* On the second date, you still need to impress her. You should consider this your second first date.

The Third Date and Beyond

She's interested, so keep her that way. Unless you've had horrible Will Smith movie *"Hitch"* type dates, where a series of bad events happened on your dates and she is going out with you out of pity, she is interested if you are on a third date. You are probably interested in her as well since you also have agreed to multiple dates. From the third date on, she is still studying you and you are learning her. As you continue with interaction and dating toward forming a relationship (if you so choose), as the perfect gentleman, a few things to remember are:

♦ Do not get too comfortable too early. By comfortable, I mean taking going on dates for granted, knowing she will say yes, dressing too casual, slacking on your flirtatious texts and so forth.

♦ The things that got her interested in you are the same things that will keep her interested in you. Continue to enhance and elevate the enjoyment she desires to have with you.

◆ After the third date, you are doing much more than impressing her. You have already done that on your previous dates. You are now more *accountable* to her as a gentleman. Opening doors, common courtesy, and fine attire she now expects and looks forward to from you as the perfect gentleman.

◆ She has come to know and expect certain things from you as a gentleman, which makes it an even greater responsibility to stay consistent in your charm and personality.

◆ In regards to kissing, touching, hugging and all the rest, do it as you both become more comfortable. Get to know her more and what she likes and let her *feel* like she is in control.

◆ I know you're wondering about sex, but I'll address that a little later in this chapter.

Ferrera Fresh Tip: Stay on her mind, even when you're not there. A nice cologne and impressive image will remind her of you, but above all be the perfect gentleman she will never forget.

Dating

Dating should always be fun. Yes, we all will have disagreements, but the overall engagement and interaction with the person you are dating should be enjoyable. If there is ever a case where you are unhappy all of the time, you may want to rethink the dating relationship. Rethinking the relationship only applies when you are in dating relationships. It is different when you are married, because at that point you should seriously work on the relationship, which will be addressed later in the section titled Perfect Gentleman Gets Married. A few notes when in a dating relationship:

- Treat your lady as much as possible. If you want, do it all the time; she's probably worth it. Remain humble and know that you are never too *manly* to have your lady treat you. Appreciate it and embrace it.

- Be open and listen to her suggestions on date ideas, but step up and just plan the full date for the two of you. Ladies love a man who takes charge and makes decisions.

- Pick her up, be on time, and know that all the respectful gentleman tips in the PGPG apply.

- Be creative. Doing things out of the ordinary will keep the spark and fun in the relationship. Hopefully, you are both open to trying new adventures, which makes the relationship exciting.

- If she is not open to the things you like, try compromising by doing things that interest her, even though you rather not do them. This may cause her to be more open to your new date ideas. If not, you may have those adventures by yourself.

- Try doing extraordinary romantic events regularly such as short weekend trips, full week vacations, a private chef dining experience, concerts and so much more. The ideas are endless and they do not always have to be expensive. Trust me, she will love it.

- The most important thing when dating is simply *invest* time with her. Yes, we all are busy, but if she is important, a gentleman makes time. Simple in-home movie dates can be just as valuable as the rooftop dinner if you plan and mix them in correctly.

> *Ferrera Fresh Tip:* You do not always have to buy her fancy gifts. Yes, she may want those things, but what she really wants is your time.

Dating Attire

The first date is the time for your attire to shine—from the colors you wear to the clothing items you choose, and *why* you choose them. Always consider where you are going when making your selections. If the restaurant, bar or club has a dress code, be aware of it before you plan your outfit and respect the place you are entering by complying with the code. Some places require dinner coats, collar shirts, or no jeans, so knowing the dress code prior to arriving is important. The last thing you want is to be dressed up, but turned away because your attire is inappropriate. When dressing for dates please know:

- Ladies appreciate a man who does not dress exactly like every other guy. Please do not always wear "the blue jeans and the black dress shirt" to every first date. The last guy she was with wore that and you look no different.

- Opt for some color in your shirt, coordinating with the seasons. For fall, choose browns and tans; for spring, sky blues or light lime greens, to name a few.

- Clean shoes are always important and they complete your outfit. Remember that most ladies are very detail oriented and are taking mental notes regarding things you may think are not important.

- Regardless of the date, time, or season, a gentleman always brings a light coat, even if it is not worn. The lady you are with may get cold or uncomfortable at some point during your date, so be prepared.

- This can also be used for unexpected weather changes such as rain and wind. This is the perfect opportunity to show you can provide and protect her, even in the simplest situation.

Ferrera Fresh Tip: Even the simplest coat or jacket can be clean, cool, and chic to complement your style.

Is it All Right to Date Multiple Women?

If you are "just dating," some ladies might be okay with you dating other ladies occasionally, as long as they are aware of it. Letting her know you see other people is not you being arrogant, but respectful. This might work for a little while or not at all because many women are territorial and want you to themselves exclusively. Eventually there will be a time when you will want to stay focused on one lady and move on from the others. However, when you are dating, always be respectful, period.

Ferrera Fresh Tip: Being a gentleman is much more than just being impressive; it's about being accountable to yourself and those around you.

What If I Cannot Make a Date Already Set

If you cannot make a date that has already been scheduled you must inform your date immediately. Regardless of how well you plan, this will eventually happen, but it should not happen often. Simply call the moment you know that you are not available and let her know. Try not to wait until the last minute unless it is a legitimate emergency. If it is a real emergency, she will understand. Initially, she might be upset, but you do not need to promise things or make it up because you cannot make it. Apologize, accept it, and start thinking about your next date as you normally would. Just don't cancel too often *with the same person*. That's just not a good look for the perfect gentleman.

When You See Her but She Hasn't Called You Back

If you happen to see a female in public that hasn't called you back yet, it might seem awkward, but relax; it's really not that awkward. There may be no particular reason as to why she has not called you back, so simply be cordial. Be a gentleman and communicate as you would with a person you haven't seen in a while. Offer a general hello, shake hands or hug and converse as you normally would. If the conversation is more than just hello and small talk, continue on if you wish and yes, you can mention that you have called and ask if she has received your message. Whatever response she gives, show no emotion. Act as if it did not bother you and carry on. If you know why she may have not called you back, be wise and just leave the topic alone.

Opening Doors

Whenever you have the opportunity to open a door for a lady, as the perfect gentleman, please do. Doors include car doors, elevator doors, shopping mall or restaurant doors and are not limited to these. As the perfect gentleman, you want to be accessible and helpful to her. The keys to opening doors as the perfect gentleman are:

- Always move in the direction the door moves. If you *pull* a door to open it, pull the door back and you move back with the door, allowing her to walk by you and through the door.

- If you must *push* a door to open it, push the door as you walk through it, ending with your back to the door you just pushed open. This allows her to walk by you, and through the door you hold open for her.

- For revolving doors, let her enter first as you help her push the door from behind in the next space.

- Some places have two sets of doors where you open the first door and then there is another door a few steps later, which can be very awkward, so don't worry about it. You may not be able to open both doors. Be creative and always open the first door.

- There may be some moments when you simply are unable to open a door for her for some odd reason like a narrow doorway or if you both are in a rush. Do not let these moments bother you. You are still the perfect gentleman.

Ferrera Fresh Tip: Opening doors for ladies demonstrates good manners. Do it as much as possible. She will appreciate you for it.

Communicating with Ladies

The most important thing when communicating with ladies is to be confident, and know that all communication skills apply.

Eye Contact

Eye contact, eye contact, eye contact! Unlike in the professional world where a short look away is appropriate, that is not the case when talking to the lady you are dating or interested in. Stay focused and look directly into her eyes as long as possible when she is talking. The best way to seem as if you are looking directly into her eyes is to focus on looking at one eye or at the bridge of her nose. She cannot tell the difference and she will feel like you are giving her undivided attention. Try it. It works and works well in conversations with others too.

Listening

Listening seems like a simple task, yet many of us have been taught how to speak but never taught how to listen. With that in mind, please know that women communicate differently than we do. It is natural for us as men to listen, find the problem and offer a solution. Interestingly, some women do not think this way. Women want details in a conversation. Better yet, they want to *give you* details. As the perfect gentleman, know that there may be times when she may just want you to *listen* to her and not necessarily offer a solution. She wants to know that it is okay to come to you when she just needs someone to talk to.

Offering listening ears to her will give her a sense of comfort. For some reason, women like that, so listen attentively. By listening to her you may need to give an occasional "Uh-huh, yea. I feel you," to let her feel like you are listening because that is what she's used to when talking to her girlfriends. However, be a man and be confident. Know when to talk, when to listen, and when to offer advice. This takes practice and as a gentleman you will interact with enough ladies in order to learn when to do these things.

Ferrera Fresh Tip: This section can be helpful even when you're not listening. Take note, I won't tell her you know this either.

Touching

Touching can be appropriate when communicating in close proximity with ladies. Women typically have a strong response to the sense of touch in good ways or in bad. If they are uncomfortable when touched by a man, it will seriously bother them. On the other hand, if a lady likes when you touch her, she will want you to do it regularly, even in small conversations when you are next to her. Be selective and choose your moments when you touch, rub or hug her.

The First Kiss

When you know that the first kiss could happen or is going to happen, relax and enjoy. It sounds very elementary, but even as men we can get carried away when attracted to someone. I do not know when, where, or how the first kiss is supposed to happen because there is no one way or perfect scenario as to when the first kiss occurs. But, I will tell you that even on a first date she has at least thought about it and has thought about if she will *ever* kiss you.

The time to pursue the first kiss is when she hints at it, shows interest, or lingers at times you know she could just leave. Now, this does not mean go full force and take a kiss from her. Be gentle, calm and cool. Gauge her actions. Eye contact is critical until you actually kiss her. Make sure you lead, but let her feel like she has control of the kiss because in actuality she does. By no means is this section of the book the "professional first kiss" or the "cool guy's kiss class." But as the perfect gentleman please know:

♦ Kissing someone for the first time can be awkward enough, so make sure you are in a private or intimate moment when the two of you are alone. This will allow her to be more comfortable.

♦ Be physically close to her, where you may already be touching, holding hands or something. It is even better if you are already facing each other.

♦ If she continues to give you more attention and you want to kiss her, gently embrace the back of her neck or chin so that she knows your intentions and has the opportunity to back away. Therefore, you can still keep your cool if she does not want to kiss you.

♦ When you do lean toward her to kiss, go extremely close to her lips, but let her kiss you. It sounds like some kind of trick, but it works. Try it.

♦ Don't be shy. Your confidence in yourself will cause her to be more attracted and comfortable with you.

♦ Keep it simple. There is no need to do too much on the first kiss. If she likes you, she will want to kiss you more at some time in the future.

♦ Once you finish your kiss, it is best not to have that awkward silence afterward. A good way to avoid this is to remember the last conversation you were having before the kiss and continue from there.

◆ If she is not interested in kissing you at that moment, accept it and carry on. Do not be embarrassed, sad or upset.

> *Ferrera Fresh Tip*: Having fresh breath, clean and non-chapped lips will make it easier for her to kiss you. Keep your mouth fresh and clean, gentlemen, so that you are always ready.

Emotions and Feelings

According to relationship specialist Alison Armstrong and her relationship program, *Celebrating Men, Satisfying Women*®, ladies have an additional body part called "feelings!" Yes, we as gentlemen have feelings as well, but women have a tendency to express their feelings more often than men do. Since we know this, as gentlemen it is our responsibility to be mindful of what we say to women and *how* we say things to them. The PGPG will not even attempt to explain a woman's feelings, but remember to be empathetic to a woman's thoughts and the sincere things she shares with you. The best thing to do is to learn and understand the person you are in a relationship with and how your actions will cause her to react. Also, be aware that a female's feelings can work to your advantage. Her high levels of emotion may cause her to like you faster

> *Ferrera Fresh Tip*: When interacting with ladies, only use her high levels of feelings and emotions to your advantage; never take advantage.

than you like her, or even cause her to show more emotion and affection around you. Regardless of the circumstance, be respectful and gentle to a woman's feelings. This is why you hold the title *"gentle" MAN*, a provider and protector that is gentle in displaying grace.

The Breakup

A relationship breakup can happen to the perfect gentleman because of a few different reasons, but that does not allow you to act inappropriately. If a breakup does happen, the perfect gentleman knows to be respectful to her at all times and:

♦ Minimize yelling and hold respectful conversations so that an agreement can be reached and you both can move on.

♦ It is a lot better to end a relationship on a good note. A breakup does not have to be a bad thing and can turn out to be better for both of you.

♦ As stated in the alcohol section, never drink just to comfort your pain after a breakup.

♦ Never feel like you have to entertain negative activities because of a breakup. You will eventually be fine if you stay positive, even in a tough situation.

♦ Stay close to friends and other gentlemen who will offer a positive environment and feedback.

♦ Stay positive in knowing you will get over it.

Ferrera Fresh Tip: It may be even better to talk about the relationship and growth before just going into a breakup. Communication and explanation can solve many misunderstandings for both parties.

The Makeup

A relationship makeup is a lot easier and a lot more enjoyable. It is almost as if the relationship has a new start or rejuvenation. As a gentleman there are a few things to keep in mind when the makeup happens.

+ Forgive and move past whatever caused the breakup in the first place, which will make the relationship fun again.

+ Do not overdo it. Start the makeup as if it were a new relationship and build from there.

+ You might want to do something nice for her just to remind her why she was interested in you in the first place and then carry on as the perfect gentleman.

+ You do not need to buy expensive makeup gifts or do anything that you would not do ordinarily. This will just remind her of the reason you gave her the gift (why you broke up), rather than just the enjoyment of the gift.

+ If she was wrong in the relationship breakup, accept it. Do not hold it against her or bring it up regularly.

+ If you were wrong in the relationship breakup, make sure you do not make the same mistake again.

+ Remember to forgive yourself. We all make mistakes, but if you have the opportunity to be in the relationship again, do it right.

Ferrera Fresh Tip: If you are in a relationship with a history of breakups to always make up, you should just consider staying together and work on the relationship.

Gift Giving

Gift giving is not always an easy task when dealing with women, considering they are all different and enjoy different things. This is key: Make sure you know and understand the person you are with. Gifts are more important to some women than others. Study her, what she likes, where she shops and the things she talks about. This will help you choose the appropriate gift. Gifts do not always have to be elaborate, but should be well

Ferrera Fresh Tip: You should know her work address so you can send gifts and flowers to her office periodically.

thought out. As your relationship grows, your gift giving may grow as well. Be considerate, respectful and give with joy and your gift will be well received.

ROSE ETIQUETTE AND REFERENCE

Rose Color	Color Symbolizes	Use These Roses When...
Red	Love, Passion	You love someone or in love with someone.
Pink	Admiration, Appreciation, Gladness, Thank you	Pink is the most versatile rose and can be used on a variety of occasions—thank you, love, or just because.
Yellow	Friendship, Happiness, Joy, Welcome Back	Perfect for birthdays, friends, coworkers, or visiting someone.

Rose Color	Color Symbolizes	Use These Roses When...
White	Purity, Love, Reverence, Honor	A great alternative to red. Also for mothers, in-laws, and those older than you. White and red roses together represent unity.
Lavender	Love at First Sight, Enchantment or Magic	You have fallen in love with someone and you're sincere. Use them occasionally and with discretion.
Orange	Enthusiasm and Desire	There is a something exciting, a great accomplishment, or something new.
Peach	Sincerity and Gratuity	Great for business gifts, professional recognition days, such as Secretary's Day or Teacher's Appreciation.

Finances and a Lady

If you're only in a dating relationship, your finances are none of her business. The perfect gentleman is private about expenses on the ladies and never needs to flaunt and show off the fancy tips, purses or gifts he purchases for a lady. As a gentleman, you should treat her and reward her as you choose to, but it should not be with the intent to show off. She also does not need to know the dollars you make, your salary or anything else, if you choose not to share it with her. That is your personal business and only becomes her business as you get closer to marriage. When married, or planning to marry, your money is her information. Share it, talk about it, and plan with it.

If questions come up in conversation at a time when you wish not to share, simply tell her that. For example, "I appreciate your respect to ask and not assume, but I'd rather not share that with you at the moment. I feel that I could possibly share information with you at a later date, but not as of yet." This says to her that she is worthy of having that information, but it is also a respectful decline, which she should respect. Use

Ferrera Fresh Tip: Dating can be expensive, but it does not always have to be. Your creativity in dating will get you farther with her than will your money.

that type of decline, when you feel appropriate and share your financial information with her when you are ready to do so.

The Perfect Gentleman Gets Married

Because of the grace you embody as a gentleman, there will come a time when you may *choose* to get married. There is emphasis on *choose* because you can still be the perfect gentleman, even if you are not married. When you do find the lady that complements your style as a gentleman, is willing to help you improve more and a woman who you love and care for, you may want to consider marriage. The rewards of life are greater when you are with a woman who *complements* you, and you both are now one working as a team to achieve greatness.

Never forget when married that all the same rules apply as when you were dating. Continue to plan dates, flirt, and remember that all the same things you did to get her interested will make her continually appreciate you. When married, the perfect gentleman knows:

◆ Communication is far more important when married than when you were just dating. Everything should be talked about, and many subjects should be talked about prior to marriage such as money, sex, and children, to name a few.

◆ Everything should be discussed continuously through a marriage relationship because life plans change and you are a man that should often take the lead!

◆ Know the personality of your spouse. Know the right times to give her space, as well as know when to ask for space from her. Talk about this. You are no longer "just dating" and can't just leave without saying anything.

◆ Let her know when you want solo time. There will be times you want to just watch a football game or do work and it is fine to let her know that.

◆ Be a helper. In order to be a good leader you must be willing to do things that you want others to do. Cooking and cleaning are not only a woman's job. As the perfect gentleman, your contributions will be greatly appreciated.

◆ Know your responsibilities and roles and complete them. Yes, there are different roles you should plan in your relationship, which must be discussed with your spouse.

◆ As relationship specialist Alison Armstrong suggests, in marriage remember to *plan* sex. With the business of life, we both can take sex for granted in marriage, but it is important to *invite* her to bed with you.

There so much more that could be written in this section, but just remember to keep learning and continue to be the perfect gentleman.

> *Ferrera Fresh Tip:* Stay focused only on your wife. As a gentleman you will always be around women and women will always be attracted to you.

The Perfect Gentleman and Family

As the gentleman with your own family, you are the head and the leader. Your wife and everyone else should respect you, your knowledge and persona just as much as you respect them. Yes, you are the provider and protector of the family, even if the lady "technically" brings home more income. Make sure to talk about this and do not let it bother either of you if there is an understanding. As the family man, being the perfect gentleman is at a higher level because you are now providing and protecting children along with a woman. There is not much

> *Ferrera Fresh Tip:* Listening to ladies can be fun and sometimes not so fun. Either way, your ability to listen with your ears will be priceless in her eyes.

more information to learn; just apply all your characteristics you already know. They are counting on you.

The Perfect Gentleman and Sex

I am sure some may have picked up this book for this section alone and have been waiting to read how the perfect gentleman handles sex. Sorry to burst your bubble, but this is not a how-to sex guide. A gentleman understands that sex is designed for married couples. So married gents, embrace and take action in treating your wife to an enjoyable experience. Bachelors, take notes and be prepared. The information in this section of the PGPG comes directly from research, women and relationship specialist Alison Armstrong, who has a wealth of information for men on sex. I will share a few important aspects that are necessary for the perfect gentleman and sex. If sex does happen prior to marriage, there are a few things the perfect gentleman should know:

- *Most* women cherish and have more mental and emotional feeling behind sex than we do.

- The physical *sex* activity they enjoy, but the touching, kissing, connection and intimacy, most of the time, is what she also enjoys.

- Although this is not always the case, be conscious of the intimacy she desires and touch her as much as possible.

- Once you are in the *sex* moment never stop touching her. Whether it is your body, a hand or even a fingertip to her body, never stop touching her while having sex.

- Kiss. Yes, you have to kiss most women during inter-course. Kissing enhances interaction with females. So kiss her all over, especially her lips.

- Talk about your intercourse beforehand. Not *right* before, but in a sincere adult relationship conversation. Know what she likes as well as explain what you like. Talk during as well. Some ladies enjoy talking during intercourse, which can make the experience more enjoyable.

- You must have "foreplay," the touching, feeling, kissing and so forth that leads up to sex.

- Gents, you have to call the day after, even if you are leaving out of town or you are busy. There is no other option. Good sex or bad sex, happy or unhappy, you have to *call.*

- If she does not answer, that is fine, but you did your part as a gentleman and it puts her at ease after you've had sex.

This section can go on forever, but I'll leave it to you married folk to write your own enjoyable chapter.

Ferrera Fresh Tip: Sex may be enjoyable to both of you, but may be enjoyable for different reasons. As the perfect gentleman, be aware of that and make the experience enjoyable for the both of you.

AWKWARD MOMENTS WITH LADIES

Caught Cheating

First off, do not cheat on her! However, if you make a mistake and get caught cheating, your gentleman characteristics of communication, interaction, and sincerity will have to be at their highest. She may or may not forgive you, but please learn and avoid the same situation from happening again. If you get caught cheating, the perfect gentleman knows:

- You eventually have to tell the truth. Honesty will avoid a ton of confusion in any relationship.

- Answer the questions she asks and that is all. Spare her the pain of your mishaps and be respectful to her as a lady.

- Never bring anyone else down or blame anyone else for your cheating mistakes. A gentleman accepts responsibility and has to accept the consequences as well.

- If you make a mistake and are unfaithful and you do not get caught, stop immediately so you do not get caught. It is up to you if you want to confess to her. If it will relieve a mental burden on you to do so, go ahead. But always repent, forgive yourself, and stop doing it.

- Be sincere. Apologize and move on. Remember to forgive yourself in order to not carry any harmful mental burdens.

She Lies or Cheats

When a female lies or cheats it may feel as if your characteristics as the perfect gentleman have gone to waste. However, it is important to remember that there may be times when certain ladies are not fit for you. If a woman does cheat on you in a relationship, it can be hurtful, but it is good to know that you will eventually feel better. Depending on how you find out, the situation and your relationship status can determine the impact it has on each gentleman. It is best to talk about the situation maturely so you can have a better understanding of the situation. If this happens to the perfect gentleman always remember:

- Control yourself and emotions so that you are not rude and do not act inappropriately.

- Unfortunately, you should try to find out *why*. At least, if you did anything wrong you can learn. If there's no genuine reason, just remember every woman is not appropriate for the perfect gentleman.

- Take time to gather yourself and thoughts. That time may be short or long, depending on the gentleman.

- Do not intimidate or scare her by yelling and carrying on in a rude manner. Yes, it may be worth a yell, but do your best to keep cool. (It's easier said than done, I know.)

- Accept the fact that it has happened and make a decision about the relationship. Whatever you decide, you must forgive and carry on as the perfect gentleman.

Ferrera Fresh Tip: It is okay for a man to cry over a woman in good situations or bad. The perfect gentleman is confident enough to embrace his emotions.

Divorce for Someone You Know

When someone close to you, male or female, goes through a divorce, there is not much you need to initiate. However, it is nice for you as a gentleman to be available to console, comfort and assist them with positive, encouraging words, and to listen. It is also appropriate if you are friends with both the male and female in the divorce to still interact with them respectfully. Do not become rude or disassociate yourself with one person because of the other person in the divorce. For example, invite them to your personal events, if you choose to. It is also polite to inform both of them individually that the other person may attend an event. Being friends with both people who are in the middle of a divorce can be very awkward, but it is important to continue to be the perfect gentleman with each person.

Divorce for You

Divorce may happen for one reason or another, even though it is best to try to work on the marriage. Seek professional counseling and even consider consulting with close people you know that have been married for a long time. Long will be relative to you, but I recommend discussing with a married couple that has been married for more than 25 years. Divorce should be the absolute last resort, even in the worst situation you can think of.

Even as the perfect gentleman there is no easy way of going through the process of a divorce, so humble yourself and get it done. All the communication and interaction skills apply in this situation as would any other. If there are children involved in the relationship, do your best to be a part of their lives, especially young men. There are just some things that boys must learn from a man. It is also important to complete the process of paperwork consistently and timely so there are no unnecessary holdups. Throughout the divorce process respect everyone from your wife, to attorneys, even if everyone is not as cordial as you are.

Awkward Conversations with Ladies

Awkward conversations with ladies are bound to happen sooner or later and they will *need* to happen so that you can learn about each other. Conversations such as past relationships, number of past sexual partners, STDs, personal experiences, rape, abuse or other topics can be extremely hard to deal with and talk about. Depending on how well the relationship is will determine how and when the conversations will occur. There is no exact timeline to follow or instructions on where these topics and conversations should happen. But around the four to five month time frame of a *sincere* dating relationship is when you may notice these conversations begin to come up. Although, depending on the relationship, these topics could come up earlier or later. Also, one topic may require more than one conversation. A few tips when in awkward conversations with the person you date are:

◆ Be mature. At least do not make any judgments directly in her face or be disrespectful.

◆ Listen, speak, and be honest. Be prepared for the worst and make your decisions accordingly, as she will.

◆ Try to minimize facial expressions as much as possible when talking and listening. You do not want to make the conversation any more uncomfortable than it already is with your non-verbal expressions.

◆ If you do not want to know, do not ask. You should, however, want to know information about the person you are interested in dating. Knowing about the person you are dating includes knowing the good as well as the bad.

◆ During the awkward conversation ask your questions, respond to questions that are asked of you and do not evade the issue.

- Be empathetic and respectful at all times since you do not know her complete past, present or who she is becoming. These conversations are simply a part of life where you are learning about her.

> *Ferrera Fresh Tip:* Honesty will avoid any confusion that could happen in the future. It might not always be the easiest option, but it is the right option. Go with it.

Awkward Hitting From a Woman

If a lady ever hits you disrespectfully or becomes abusive to you, try to bear with it as much as possible. It may just be an emotional moment, but never let it get out of control. This is a very awkward moment for the perfect gentleman and often the best thing to do is leave the environment for a while. Let her calm down and then return when appropriate. You never want to react or respond in a harmful way to the woman. If you ever make the mistake where abuse becomes a problem to women, please humble yourself, talk to someone you trust and get help.

Calling When You Haven't Spoken in a While

When you haven't talked to a woman in a while, calling can be a very humbling situation. The first thing you should do is plan why you are calling. In other words, determine if you are just calling to say hello, calling to offer comfort to bad news, or calling for another reason. Whatever the reason for your call, stay focused and accomplish that purpose. It may be an awkward conversation at first, but be genuine in your reason for calling.

If you are interested in dating her again, it is best to start with a friendship, if she is open to it, and build from there. Plan simple dates and general hangouts, short phone conversations and treat her as you would a new person of interest. It may turn out to be just that, a friendship, which is completely fine. You may not know her relationship status or any changes that may have happened in her life since you last dated, and you may have to accept simply reconnecting. If there is a voice machine when you call her, leave a message and respond accordingly with proper phone call etiquette. Keep it brief and communicate with confidence.

"Is This Your Girlfriend?"

There will probably come a time when you are in public or in front of a group of people and someone asks, *"Is this your girlfriend?"* When the lady you are with is not your girlfriend, your cool has to be sky high, and you have to be creative in your answer. I mean, you do not want to claim a girl who is not yours or make her feel like she is not worthy enough to be your girlfriend. It's an awkward situation, I know. You do not want to ruin the chance for her to eventually be that person. A few ideas that can help when this happens are:

- Say "Well, the least I can say is that she's the person I get the privilege of hanging out with…"

- Give a light chuckle and say "Not at the moment, but I'll let her answer that question at a later date…"

- Another option is to say "It may eventually be the case, but for now, I just get the chance to have a wonderful date with a great person…"

- If the lady you're with is really just a friend that you are hanging out with at the moment, then just say that. Whatever answer you choose, be cool, be joyous, and do not be embarrassed.

- The key to leaving this situation is to answer the question, glance at the lady and change the topic.

> *Ferrera Fresh Tip:* The perfect gentleman knows never to put another gentleman or lady in this awkward situation. If you want to know, ask at a later time in private.

I Just Want to be Friends

When a female you are interested in just wants to be "friends," it may be disappointing, but it can work to your advantage. The reason being is that you might now have a good looking female friend that can give you insight when dealing with other ladies in the future. The key in this situation is to be open and listen. When she just wants to be friends the perfect gentleman knows:

- Hear her thoughts as to *why*. What caused her to feel that way? Try to find out if there was anything done wrong on your part so that you can continue to improve as a gentleman.

- Communicate how you feel and do explain if you'd rather be in a relationship with her. Be bold and confident in what you ask and what you say.

+ If she seriously just wants to be friends, accept it. Continue as her friend and as the perfect gentleman.

Ferrera Fresh Tip: Even if she just wants to be friends it can be to your benefit to maintain friendships with good looking females you have dated in the past, since they may help you improve as a man.

When you, as the perfect gentleman, want to only be friends with a female you have dated, it can be tricky. However, you *can* bow out gracefully. I wish I could share with you a tried and true formula that always works, but that is not the case because every woman's feelings are different. After you know for sure that you just want to be friends, let her know that. If she is a true lady and you have been a gentleman thus far, she should appreciate it and you can carry on. A few things to remember in this situation are:

+ Be sincere and do not touch, flirt, hint or entice her. Be a friend since being a friend is what you are suggesting.

+ You will need to be prepared to have a discussion. You will have to listen to thoughts, but stand confidently in your belief, if that is how you feel. Women will do things to keep you if she wants to.

+ If you are not certain as to what relationship you want with her, consider talking about it with her in a respectful manner.

Ferrera Fresh Tip: There should be no such things as friends with benefits. Always respect women and be mature in your decisions. You are the perfect gentleman.

INTERESTING ENJOYABLE MOMENTS WITH LADIES

Shopping with a Lady

Walking around and shopping with a lady is not the most exciting thing to do, but she may like it. Carrying her shopping bags is up to you and you do not have to do it. However, if she needs help or you have the opportunity to help her, do so. I know it is not the coolest thing to be holding a lingerie shopping bag, but help for a moment. I hope that while shopping with her she does not ask you to do too much rather than be present, but as a gentleman always remember:

* Try not to hold her purse for a long time. If she asks you to hold her purse as she does something, yes, you have to do it. Hopefully you know not to put it on your shoulder like she does.

* If she asks you how something looks on her, be selective and careful with your choice of words. One way of being polite if you do not like something she tries on is to always compliment her on how pretty *she* is. Then comment on whatever the item is. If you like something, just tell her with confidence. That's easy!

* If you are shopping for items for her, add your input selectively. Most women know what they want and they just want you to confirm something they already like or don't like.

* If you are shopping for items for you, make sure you have input. Pick out your own clothes, accessories and so forth. You're the perfect gentleman, so own your style and use the style tips in Chapter 3 as needed.

* A great way to make the shopping experience better is to take breaks. Say to her, "I'm going over here for a bit. I'll

be back in a few minutes." Then just walk to a different area, get a pretzel or just relax and return. This break is priceless!

♦ Even when she says you are about to leave, just mentally prepare for a little while longer and plan accordingly.

Ferrera Fresh Tip: Shopping with a lady can be an adventure, mentally prepare yourself for it.

Driving with Ladies

When driving a car while females are present and you are the driver, make sure they are comfortable. This applies to the music being played, the temperature of the car and anything else that will cause her to be at ease. You may want to drive a little slower too, so she feels safe and she doesn't complain. If you are with a person who always has something to say about your driving, the best thing to do is to tune her out so you can stay focused. Agree with her sometimes, even though you may think differently, just so you can move on.

Ferrera Fresh Tip: Ask before rolling down the windows with a lady in the car. Not only do they get cold more often than we do, but also you do not want to mess up her hair from the wind blowing.

Walking with a Lady

Since you may be dating and she shows interest in you walking side-by-side or hand-in-hand is not always a bad thing. Walk with her proudly. Hold hands, let her hold you, and put your arm around her at times when it is cold, for comfort or just because.

It is proper for a man to walk closest to the street side as a sign of protection. But this is not to protect her from cars; it is to offer a protection from wind, water or anything else that can come from the street side. The most important thing to remember when walking side by side with a lady is to go with the flow. You never want to ruin a moment because you want to be "technically" appropriate on where you should be walking or standing. Just enjoy the moment. She will appreciate that more. A few hints and tricks when walking with a lady are:

- Most women, if they are interested in you, will eventually want to hold your hand or be close to you since you are already a gentleman.

- As you walk with her be conscious of your walking stride. Men tend to naturally walk faster than women. She also may have on high heels or shoes that will cause her to walk a bit slower than normal.

- When walking with a woman and a man is walking toward you, move in a direction where he can walk past on your side and not hers, if possible.

- If another woman is passing, or group of ladies are passing you both, it is best for you and the lady you are with to move out of *their* way and bring your lady slightly closer to you.

- Keep these notes in mind when you are walking alone and see other daters and adjust accordingly.

> *Ferrera Fresh Tip:* When you do not want to hold hands with her in public, a gentleman's trick is to put your hands in your pockets, hold a cell phone, or do something to occupy your hands.

Public Display of Affection (PDA)

Public display of affection is such a female thing to do, but a gentleman welcomes it. If the woman you are with is your girlfriend or spouse, you will *have* to do it at times. It is perfectly fine to display your affection to her in public and it is actually cool. It shows that the lady you're with is not embarrassed of being seen with you in public. However, if she does not show you PDA, it does not mean she is embarrassed of you. As the perfect gentleman remember:

◆ Keep it brief! Your affection or long hugging and kissing are for private time between the two of you.

◆ If you want PDA, start with small touches or an arm around her shoulders and see how she responds.

◆ One way to subtly avoid PDA is to keep your hands busy. Hold your keys or a cell phone that can occupy your hands. If she really wants to touch you, she will wrap her arms around your arm as her escort, showing you her interest.

◆ If you are with your wife the *cool* factor does not apply. You should be able to confidently hug and kiss her whenever you want. Just be conscious of the few tips listed above.

Ferrera Fresh Tip: Sometimes it's a little bit cooler to have her hold on to your arm as an escort rather than being locked up hand-in-hand.

Cool Date Ideas

Dinners, movies and coffee dates are classic and will not go out of style anytime soon. But as the perfect gentleman, be creative in your date selection. Let her know why she is with you or why she *should* be with you. Talk with other gents and ladies. Share ideas and experiences and add them to your database of cool date ideas. Here are a dozen cool dates to add to the ones you already know.

◆ Ice skating or roller skating

◆ Specialty dancing lessons

◆ Beach picnic

◆ Miniature golfing

◆ Billiards or chess

◆ Cooking together

◆ Theme parks

◆ Lingerie shopping

◆ Specialty historic tours

◆ Wine tasting

◆ Pottery making

◆ Outdoor activities

Ferrera Fresh Tip: Some dates may be cheesy to you but could be appealing to your date. Use them at your discretion and don't forget that staying home for the evening can be a valuable date as well.

Text Message and Email Flirting

Gentlemen, only use text messages and email flirting to your advantage and never because you are shy. When you are busy, cannot talk, or just want to let her know you are thinking of her, use text, email, and social media flirting, occasionally. You will stay on her mind and make her look forward to your next personal interaction. As the perfect gentleman remember a few tips for technology flirting are:

- Do not use it as your only means of communication and flirting. The things you may say on text can often be said on the phone or in person. Flirting with her in person will allow you to see her response and determine if you should do more or not.

- Try not to make official dates over text messages or email. Exceptions are if text and email are the only way and you are already involved in some type of dating relationship. A phone call or planning future dates in person is better and more personal than text messaging.

- Flirtatious text messages are great just before you walk into a meeting, before you hop on a plane or when you know you can't talk for a while. A quick text allows you to stay on her mind, even when you cannot talk.

- Text messaging can also put a smile on her face as if you are there, even though you are not.

- Use her text message responses to spark new conversations when you are with her in person.

- Don't overdo it. Text messages can be fun and also overwhelming. Sometimes it might be better to wait and talk to her on the phone. Know the person you are with and respond accordingly with your text message dialogue.

> *Ferrera Fresh Tip:* No matter how long you've been dating, or even married to her, never stop flirting. If it gives her the slightest smile, it is all worth it.

Flirtatious Touches

When you get small touches and playful hits from a female, that is a good thing. Accept it and take note that she may be flirting with you and that this can build on a fun relationship. Remember, though, a gentleman never ever hits a lady.

Meeting Her Friends

Whether you know it or not, her friends are checking you out long before they even meet you. Because of your gentlemanly characteristics, she has already talked about you to her friends and they already have mental ideas about you, good or bad. The first time you meet her friends just be the gentleman that you are. When you meet her friends, male or female, for the first time remember:

- The engagement is all about the friends, not really about your girl. The person you are dating already likes you. Now make her friends smile, be courteous to them and get them to like you too.

- This will allow you to be alone with the person you are dating without her friends having a conniption.

◆ As a gentleman, you really will not need to try too hard for her friends to like you. Besides, if they end up not liking you, it doesn't matter. The woman you are dating is the most important and if you make her happy, that is all that really counts.

> *Ferrera Fresh Tip:* There will be times when you meet some of her friends who approve of you and some that disapprove. Don't let the disapprovals bother you. You are dating her, not her friends.

Meeting Her Parents

Meeting her parents is a lot easier than you may think because you are already a perfect gentleman. Some fathers and mothers will have a bias toward their daughter but most simply want the best for their daughter and rightfully so. If you continue to display yourself as the perfect gentleman, they will get to know you with time. Be yourself, talk, shake hands, hug, listen, learn and apply all proper manners and etiquette in any situation.

> *Ferrera Fresh Tip:* There's nothing to worry about when meeting her parents or family members. If she is into you, the parents will at least want to know about you as well.

Female Friends

Having ladies as just close friends is great because they can help you with ideas and tips from a female's perspective, which will help you advance with the ladies you date. As the perfect gentleman, it is so appropriate to have good lady friends and treat them with the same respect you would treat anyone else.

Although a whole book could be written about how the perfect gentleman interacts with women, within this chapter you have gained more than enough fuel to be charming and graceful with ladies. Use the information to your advantage and add to your knowledge based on the many experiences of life. Regardless of the good, bad, amazing or uneventful experiences you have with the ladies, know that they are truly a gift. Care for them, love them, appreciate them and respect them. They are worth it. I promise.

9
The Perfect Gentleman
is not a Perfect Human

As stated earlier, the Perfect Gentleman's Pocket Guide is not a cure-all to being perfect, since no human on earth is perfect. However, this book is your resource to life's awkward situations that can guide you through continuously being the perfect *gentleman,* even when mistakes happen. Yes, we all make mistakes, but the perfect gentleman knows to *learn* from his mistakes and minimizes the same mistakes from occurring continuously. When a mistake happens, the perfect gentleman knows when he is wrong and accepts it. In this chapter you will find helpful tips for handling unexpected mistakes and errors that are bound to happen. You will find advice on what to do and say and how to respond and follow up in order to keep your composure.

Apologizing

What one person may think is wrong may seem like the norm to another. Keep that in mind and be open to the feelings and ideas of other people. Also recognize that the severity of the mistake may call for a greater apology than others. If you have simply spilled a glass of milk, a simple apology is fine. Clean it up and move on. If you hurt someone's feelings because of *Ferrera Fresh Tip*: In any situation, tell the truth. The truth, at times, may hurt, but it prevents confusion in the future. your mistake, a genuine apology is a must, and should be presented differently than your apology about spilled milk.

Making an Apology

♦ The most important thing to remember when making an apology is to be sincere. It is worst to give a phony "I'm sorry" than not saying anything at all. It is even disrespectful to the person receiving the apology.

♦ Whenever possible, apologize verbally. The apology will be more personal and delivered with more clarity when spoken. An email or text message can get lost in translation and cause further confusion. Text message apologies can only fly for simple mistakes.

♦ Ditch the long, drawn out, over exaggerated apologies. They can sometimes be taken as being insincere. Get to the point and move forward.

♦ I wish there was a set time limit on how long an apology should be, but there isn't one. Say what needs to be said in order to get your point across.

♦ There's not always a need to say, "How can I make it up to you?" Some mistakes cannot be corrected. What has been done is done. Just be more cautious to keep and rebuild trust and confidence of that person.

♦ If you would like to do something for a person to make it up, feel free, but it is not required.

> *Ferrera Fresh Tip:* There is no need to apologize three or more times for the same mistake. Say it once and move on. After a while, it just becomes useless talk.

When to Make an Apology

The best time to apologize is as soon as you know you've made a mistake, no matter how big or small. It shows others you are mindful of your actions and they may be more willing to forgive. It will also be fresh in their mind and can cause less harm when addressed immediately.

> *Ferrera Fresh Tip:* Choose the words in your apology very carefully. Remember, it is often how you say your words that will have more impact than the words alone.

What to Say

There is a ton of ways to apologize and it is really your personal preference on the words you choose to use. "I'm sorry, my bad, my fault, excuse me, please forgive me, I apologize" are just a few on a long list. Keep in mind the short modern style apologies, "my bad," or "my fault," are for minor errors, while more severe mistakes require a more formal apology. In more severe cases, start with "I apologize…" Regardless, choose your words wisely. An apology is still communication and all rules apply as stated before. Eye contact, *how* you say it and so forth all play a part in your delivery.

When to Write an Apology

An apology should be written when a severe error has been made or the person or persons cannot be contacted by phone. This is most common in business engagements and professional interactions. If a meeting was missed or a call not returned, or simple task was not done, a quick apology email may work. If there is a large number of people to contact or that were impacted because of your major error, you should write a formal apologetic letter.

What If I Don't Think I Was Wrong

If you don't think you were wrong, respectfully explain that to the person. As stated earlier, we all are different and what may seem wrong to one person can be taken differently by another. A few ways to address this situation are:

- "If you feel that I have made a mistake, I do apologize. However, I believe that…." After this, state your feelings and opinion. Accept a little discussion, but stay calm and do not open an argument.

- "I'm sorry you feel this way…"

Ferrera Fresh Tip: If a lady you have a relationship with expects an apology and you don't think one is warranted, be cautious. Know her personality, but still express your opinion or the issue will never be solved.

When a Person Does Not Apologize

When a person makes a mistake and does not apologize, it can be more annoying than the wrong action itself. As the perfect gentleman, do your best to not let it interfere with the rest of your day or event. When you have calmed down and you have a moment to communicate to that person, share with him or her how you feel in the hopes they acknowledge their mistake. Do not force others to apologize, but as the perfect gentleman remember to forgive. Life is just too short to hold grudges against others. Do not allow people to take advantage of your kindness by continuing to be rude, but do forgive.

I Realized I was Wrong Afterwards

Realizing you were wrong after the incident has happened can occur to all of us, so do not feel bad and make the situation worse for yourself. Simply correct the error if you are able to correct it and apologize as soon as possible. Remember to reference the tips stated above and handle the situation appropriately. If you know the person very well, contact them immediately. If not, doing so during a reasonable time of day is appropriate.

Forgive Yourself

Forgiving yourself can be one of the most challenging things to do. There are countless people living today with grief and strife and experiencing heart attacks and depression because they have not forgiven themselves for past transgressions. Do not live like this. Not forgiving yourself is too hard on your mind and body, and will ultimately cause you to miss other experiences in life, without even noticing. In life we will experience traumatic events ranging from cheating in a relationship, to cases of death, but it's important to forgive yourself and get on with your life. You cannot change the past, but you can change how you respond to it, now and in the future. Forgive yourself. You are worth it.

Ferrera Fresh Tip: Stay positive. Live, learn and enjoy life.

10

The Perfect Gentleman
Knows How To. . .

As the perfect gentleman it is very appropriate to offer cash tips as an additional thank you for someone who provides service to you. As you consider your tip amount, it is important to remember that the tip you give is based on your discretion. Depending on the quality of service rendered, you can give more or less than the suggested amount. If someone refuses your tip in a polite way, do not be offended. Some places do not allow their employees to accept tips, so do not force people to do so. On occasion, you can say to a person, "Please accept it." However, do not demand or force people to accept your tip. Below you will find a few guidelines for giving tips.

GRATUITY RECOMMENDATIONS

Situation	Percent	Dollar
Eating Out & Dining	15-30 %	Use %
Haircuts & Shaves	10-20 %	$2-5
Valet Parking	10-20 %	$2-5
Coat Check	Use $ Amount	$1-3
Shoe Shine	10-15 %	$1-3
Restroom Attendant	Use $ Amount	$1-2
Bellhop Luggage	Use $ Amount	$5-10
Car Wash	10-25 %	$2-5
Golf Caddy	10-30 %	$5-50
Air Port Skycap	Use $ Per Bag	$1-2
Manicure	10-20 %	$2-5
Pedicure	15-20 %	$3-7
Spa and Massage	10-15 %	$5-25
Hotel Housekeeping	Use $ per night	$2-5

Polish Shoes

1. Wipe the shoes with a cloth or large dust brush to rid any dust from the shoe. Occasionally remove the shoelaces to polish the tongue.

2. Use a shoe polish that matches the original color of the shoe. Use a few drops of water to make the polish moist.

3. Dab the shoe polish brush or toothbrush into the polish.

4. Use small circular motions to massage the polish into the scuffed areas of the leather and heel. Repeat steps 3 and 4 until the shoe is an even color.

5. Let the polish dry, which should take about two to three minutes.

6. Use some type of shoe shine to give the finishing touches after your polish.

Neckties

There is a wide part and a small part to a necktie.

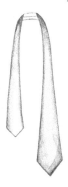

HOW TO TIE A WINDSOR KNOT

Start by placing the tie around your collar with the small part about 4-5 inches above your waistline, since you will be using more of your tie and you do not want it to be too short.

1. Take the wide part and wrap it around the small part, while bringing the wide part under and through the space closest to your neck.

2. Now return it over the top to the same side.

3. Now bring the wide part to the other side remaining at the bottom.

4. Bring the wide part over the top, through the space closest to your neck and to the opposite side remaining underneath.

5. Wrap the wide part across to the front of the knot.

6. Bring the wide part underneath and through the space closest to your neck.

7. Then bring the wide part through the front to finish the tie.

8. Tighten, form, and straighten the knot at your collar to your liking and you're set.

243

Half-Windsor Knot

1. Place the tie around your collar with the small part about 2-3 inches above your waistline.

2. Take the wide part and cross it over the small part and around back to the same side.

3. Then bring it over and through the space close to your neck and bring it to the other side at the bottom. Wrap the wide part over the front to form the knot.

4. Bring it under and through the space close to your neck.

5. Finish by bringing the tie down and through the front to tie the knot.

6. Form and straighten to your liking.

Four-in-Hand

(See page 77.)

Bowties

(See page 78.)

How to Tie a Scarf

1. Fold the scarf in half along the width.

2. Drape the scarf around your neck.

3. Insert the two ends of the scarf through the loop where the scarf is folded.

4. Adjust the tie close to your neck as you would a necktie. Make sure it's to your liking and you're set.

Fold Pocket Square

2point

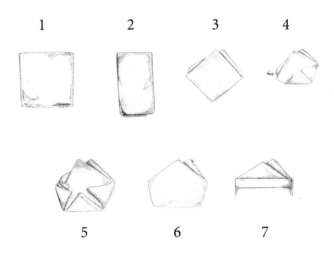

1   2   3   4

5   6   7

Multi point

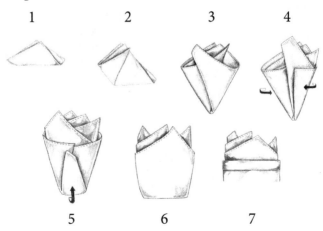

1   2   3   4

5   6   7

The puff

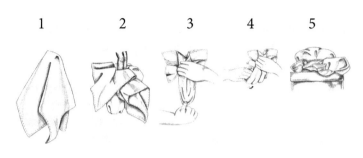

The fold

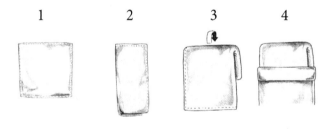

Ferrera Fresh Tip: The puff and the pocket square fold are the two easiest ways to fold a pocket square. Use these methods whenever you are in a rush when getting dressed.

CONCLUSION

As we continue upon this the enjoyment of life, it is important to know that the perfect gentleman is now in you. The characteristics of a perfect gentleman are learned, studied and enhanced. It should be known that the perfect gentleman does not hold himself higher that he ought and never rudely belittles someone in a subsidiary position. Rather, as the perfect gentleman, it is our job to enhance the lives of those around us.

The Merriam-Webster definition of etiquette is the required or acceptable decorum, rules, manners, and ceremonies of individuals in different social relations, professions, or life in general. In conjunction, the perfect gentleman's definition of etiquette is the ability to *accept* rules while displaying character and charisma among others with respect and appreciation, which allows life experiences to be more enjoyable.

It is important to know as we conclude in the final pages of the PGPG, that the perfect gentleman never stops learning. Consistent study and implementation of the perfect gentleman characteristics in this book will allow one to continually enhance personality and style, even though many of these things will be habit for you as the perfect gentleman. When these characteristics become a habit, it is important to fine tune them, which will allow them to improve even more. In addition, as the perfect gentleman many people will be watching you from near and far, seeking to learn more about this man who they intriguingly know as the perfect gentleman.

In speaking from one perfect gentleman to another, I encourage you to always display grace, character and integrity. Above all, walk, talk and interact with confidence as the perfect gentleman should. Your persona will naturally attract other respectful gentlemen and wonderful women in your life. These moments will allow you the opportunity to impact their lives for the better, even if for a short moment. This book The Perfect Gentleman's Pocket Guide is your resource for information to display yourself as the perfect gentleman, even in life's most awkward situations. Use it and allow the world to embrace your charisma and charm as the perfect gentleman you are.

Acknowledgments

I give all praise and glory to God. Thank you, Lord, for providing me with the vision to produce this work. It is through You of which all good and great things come forth.

The dedication of this book is so sincere. To my parents, at this time in my life there are no words that can express how grateful I am for you. Your wisdom, your guidance, your knowledge, your encouragement, your willingness to give and your abundant love are immeasurable. I love you both greatly.

Ed, we did it, brother! Thank you, thank you, thank you. We did not know what we were doing, but we started. I cannot thank you enough for your support and being my right hand in this journey of completing my first book. Your knowledge, creativity, and encouragement were beneficial to me more than you know. Thanks for listening to my ideas and my off-the-wall "what if's." Some of them made it and some of them didn't. I've already started writing; let's do it again.

Clara Jane, wow! Where do I start? Your artistic ability and talent are amazing! Thank you for being part of this work. It was an absolute pleasure to work with you and your positive spirit. I admire your passion for what you do as an artist. It shows in your work and I encourage you to never lose that. Imagine how many lives you are making easier with your illustrations throughout these pages.

Ricky Dorn, your leadership skills are impeccable. Your skills to *just get stuff done* will be extraordinary valuable to your continued success. Thank you for your organization in bringing the right team together to finish this project.

Brittney Fox, you're a creative genius, and I mean it. You made the cover come to life. Thanks for your creativity and ideas that enhanced *my* creativity and ideas. It is a great gift you have when you make other people around you better.

Thank you to my partners and contributors of this work. It could not have been done without you: Joan Stanford, Gemini Adams, Nkechi Ahaiwe, Jessica Tilles, The Art Institute of California, Larry Bethea, Sherry West, and Mat Guillen.

Finally, there are others who need not be named. Thank you to my mentors, coaches, partners, colleagues, extended loved ones and friends for your words of encouragement and support. The times when you saw me working, but knew not what I did. Your support of the unknown is noticed and truly appreciated. You are the ones who allowed me to use the book, put it into practice and confirm that it works. Your words, questions, comments, concerns, ideas, willingness to listen, read, reply, and simply being in my life will never be forgotten.

To the reader: Thank you for reading. I trust you enjoyed it and I am one hundred percent confident that you learned at least one thing new. And for that, my time spent was all worth it. Embrace yourself as the perfect gentleman or embrace the perfect gentleman. Thanks a bunch and tell others about this great book you just read!

About The Author

Michael Ferrera is an ambitious and focused entrepreneur from Los Angeles, California. Learning the fundamentals of business from the young age of fourteen, Michael Ferrera managed his father's music company and assisted with operations. At eighteen, while in college at the University of California Riverside studying economics, he established his first t-shirt and sweat suit clothing company with the intention of expanding his brand into a complete line of luxury menswear. As an international business professional specializing in men's fashion, Michael is currently the founder and president of Michael Ferrera Custom Clothing, a bespoke menswear company dedicated to the highest standards of custom suits, shirts and personalized accessories. Michael Ferrera currently resides in the beautiful City of Angels and lives every day with the sole purpose of enjoying life.

CPSIA information can be obtained
at www.ICGtesting.com
Printed in the USA
BVHW040806090221
599529BV00004B/424

9 780985 369804